D1357797

Berlinwalks

This is the
Henry Holt Walks Series,
which originated with
PARISWALKS *by Alison and Sonia Landes.*
Other titles in this series include:

BERLINWALKS

Peter Fritzsche
and Karen Hewitt

An Owl Book

Henry Holt and Company • New York

Henry Holt and Company, Inc.
Publishers since 1866
115 West 18th Street
New York, New York 10011

Henry Holt ® is a registered
trademark of Henry Holt and Company, Inc.

Published in Canada by Fitzhenry & Whiteside Ltd.,
195 Allstate Parkway, Markham, Ontario L3R 4T8.

Library of Congress Cataloging-in-Publication Data
Fritzsche, Peter.
Berlinwalks / Peter Fritzsche and Karen Hewitt.
p.   cm.
"An Owl book."
Includes index.
1. Berlin (Germany)—Tours.   2. Walking—Germany—Berlin—
Guidebooks.   I. Hewitt, Karen.   II. Title.
DD859.F74   1994   93-42294
914.31'5504879—dc20   CIP

ISBN 0-8050-2460-3

Henry Holt books are available for special promotions
and premiums. For details contact:
Director, Special Markets.

First Owl Book Edition—1994

Maps by Jeffrey L. Ward

Grateful acknowledgment is made to Landesbildestelle Berlin for
permission to reproduce illustrations on pages vi, xvi, 6, 13, 68,
105, 113, 129, 141.

Printed in the United States of America
All first editions are printed on acid-free paper. ∞

1   3   5   7   9   10   8   6   4   2

Frontispiece: The New Synagogue.

For Eric and Lauren

Contents

Acknowledgments

If acknowledgments were walks, we would start by thanking Nils Jacobsen, and Bruce Ostler at Fifi Oscard Agency. Then we would have to mention the obstacles on the way—those unexpected detours that add immeasurably to the journey: our son, Eric, who was born in Berlin, and our daughter, Lauren, who learned to walk (to the playground) in Berlin. To them this book is dedicated. We would also want to mention the throughway traffic, or perhaps we should say the encouraging pedestrians: Kate Doughty; Katja, Hellmut, and Sybille Fritzsche; Barbara Hewitt and John Basye; Tracy Egan; Betty Gold and Michael Kahn; and Cris Miller and Jerry Frakes. Thank you all for "going the distance," sometimes under less than ideal conditions. For imagining images, special thanks to Thomas Fritzsche. And for being in Berlin, thank you to Carol Scherer and Faustyn Plitzko.

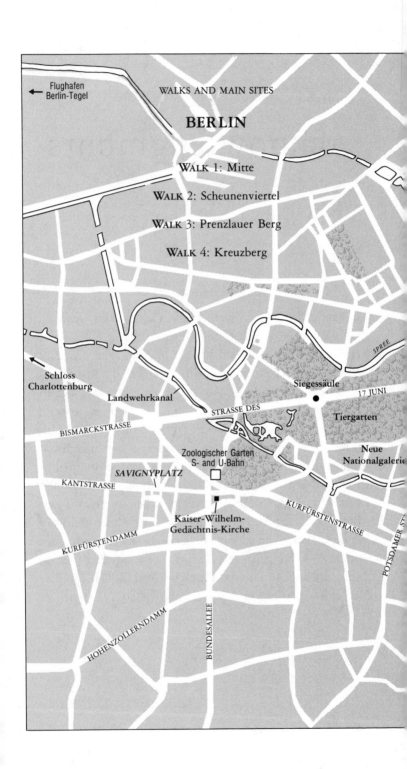

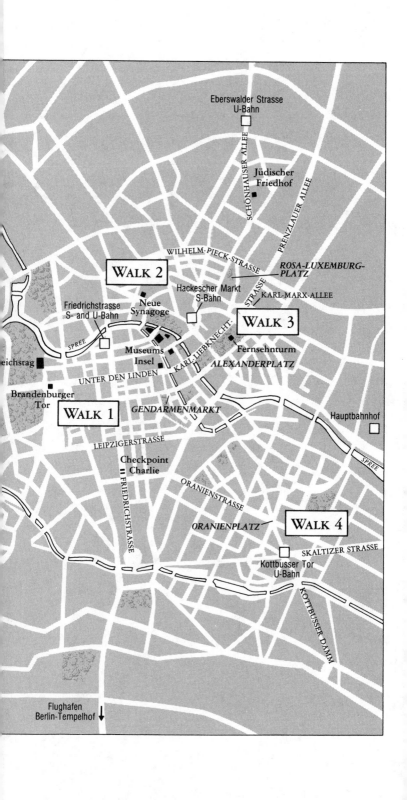

Introduction

Berlin is Europe's most modern city and, paradoxically, always has been. Berlin is not simply the new capital of a reunified Germany that is rebuilding itself on a grand scale; Berlin is also a city that visionary architects and city planners, social revolutionaries and ruling kaisers have all tried to reshape. Over the course of the last three hundred years, there always has been a new Berlin in the making, and each version has left its mark on the city. As a result, Berlin is sheathed in layers of modern history—each layer a chapter in the city's story of constant change. The four walks included in this book are designed to unwrap and reveal the traces of the city's breathtaking development.

The modern aspect of the city is all the more dominant because Berlin, unlike Vienna, Paris, or London, never was a Roman settlement, did not figure in the boisterous commercial activity of the Middle Ages, and never was the capital of a seafaring empire. This city came into its own only during the Industrial Revolution. As a relative newcomer, detractors denounced Berlin as "Parvenupolis," an ugly duckling compared to the other great cities of Europe. But growing over the course of the nineteenth century from an insignificant provincial town into a tumultuous metropolis, Berlin quickly became the focus of startling innovation in the arts and industry. Every year thousands of newcomers arrived at the city's half-dozen train stations to make their fortunes and their reputations.

The new city breathed a rich atmosphere full of excitement, quick wit, and impertinence. One hundred years ago, visitors such as Mark Twain were remarking with astonishment on the city's relentless pace of transformation and comparing it to Chicago. By 1900 the extraordinary energy of Berlin made the city the foremost intellectual center in Germany. Poets, painters, and novelists all flocked to Berlin to experience life in the big city. Berlin's lively theaters, cafes, and bawdy street life drew visitors from around the world. And while the imperial ambitions of the last kaiser, Wilhelm II, ended disastrously in World War I, Berlin continued to change in dramatic fashion. At one point in the 1920s, Berlin's master planner, Martin Wagner, forecast the need to make over the central city every twenty-five years! As a result, the cityscape juxtaposes the avant-garde with older monumental constructions.

During the Weimar Republic (1919–33), Berlin was the celebrated site of artistic innovation and architectural Bauhaus experimentation. Berlin also witnessed much of the urban misery of the Great Depression, a period of political violence and economic hardship that ended with the Nazi seizure of power in 1933. Over the twelve-year course of the Third Reich, Hitler's architect, Albert Speer, began to rebuild Berlin in National Socialist fashion, an effort that left its marks on the city. The Nazis continue to haunt Berlin in other ways as well: Buildings in which concentration-camp victims were rounded up still stand throughout the city.

This ceaseless process of destruction and reconstruction, which took place between 1890 and 1940, is physically preserved in the saw-toothed profile of Berlin streets. The massive Allied bombing in 1943–45 only sharpened the effect. Buildings across Berlin still wear bullet holes and scars from artillery fire of street-to-street fighting that took place in April 1945. After the division of Germany in 1949, East and West Berlin developed their own highly distinctive "modern" styles. The attempt of the East Germans, in particular, to demolish the pre-Communist past and advertise their new Germany has left eastern Berlin with yet another layer of history. The Cold War and the construction of the Berlin Wall in 1961 refashioned not just the physical landscape but the intellectual and artistic landscape of the city in indelible ways. Now that Berlin will become the capital of a reunited and prosperous Germany, further dramatic changes to the cityscape are inevitable.

Berlin is fascinating precisely because it is a vast archeological site of the twentieth century. It is a unique place in which the remnants of its various pasts are exposed and juxtaposed. The four walks in this book explore Berlin's history as a small medieval commercial town; as the capital of nineteenth-century Prussia; as the bustling center of an ambitious imperial Germany; as the modern dreamscape of the Weimar Republic; as the "new Rome" of the Third Reich; as the target of a fearsome Allied bombing; as the front line of the Cold War; as a divided city; and now, as the new capital of a reunited Germany.

Walk 1—Berlin Mitte: The Historic City Center—takes you into Berlin's historic city center and traditional seat of government, and to the site of two of Berlin's most famous monuments: The Brandenburger Tor and the now dismantled Berlin Wall. Beginning at Potsdamer Platz and concluding at the historic gate, the walk takes you through Checkpoint Charlie, the eighteenth-century Gendarmenmarkt, past vacant government buildings of the former East German Republic, and along the historic boulevard Unter den Linden. Encompassing over three hundred years of history—from the Prussian kings through Hitler's Reich to the present—this long walk is filled with the sweep of Germany's troubled history.

Walk 2—The Scheunenviertel: The Jewish Quarter—is a tour through Berlin's former Jewish quarter and one of

Berlin's oldest districts. Hidden behind the wall, this neighborhood fell into decline during the Cold War years, but as home to many of Berlin's poorest immigrants, it never was very prosperous to begin with. Along these once bustling streets, remnants of the sad history of Berlin's Jewish population are revealed. Today the Scheunenviertel is reviving: Galleries, cafes, and refounded Jewish schools and synagogues have given new life to old stones.

Walk 3—Prenzlauer Berg: A Proletarian District— traverses a distinctive working-class neighborhood in East Berlin. The walk begins at Alexanderplatz, the socialist-style plaza that formed part of the traditional parade route along Karl-Marx-Allee and served as a gathering spot for the hundreds of thousands of workers housed in the monochromatic apartment complexes radiating out from here. From this dated version of modern, the walk proceeds into an adjacent working-class neighborhood—one that remains essentially untouched since its construction at the end of the nineteenth century. It provides a glimpse into tenement buildings and neighborhood streets, introduces the artists and political leaders who spoke for Berlin's impoverished factory workers, and probes the realities of everyday life in former East Germany.

Walk 4—Kreuzberg: Experiments in Diversity— explores one of West Berlin's more notorious neighborhoods. The Berlin Wall once sliced through this district, isolating it from the rest of the city. As a result, a youthful alternative culture took over the abandoned apartments and factory spaces. Residents made the wall their political sounding board, and artists frequently pricked the conscience of more complacent and affluent West Berliners. Kreuzberg is also the site of massive postwar housing reform attempts and home to many of Berlin's Turkish guest workers. It is a vibrant area now, but with the wall's disappearance, the neighborhood is again centrally located and is sure to experience massive transformation in the coming years.

No doubt your choice of walks will depend on your

particular interests, but we encourage you to read through all of them since, taken together, they form a composite picture of Berlin's history. The first three walks are located in what was formerly East Berlin, which might seem an odd decision but many of the significant events in Berlin—and German—history took place on what was once the east side of the wall. In preparing to write this book, we found it exhilarating to explore these sites more thoroughly and were astonished at the rapid pace of change. It is hard for visitors who never saw East Berlin when the wall was in place to imagine how desolate the streets once looked. And because things are changing so fast, navigating through these sections of the city may be difficult. Sometimes entire blocks are covered in scaffolding as buildings are repaired; or streets are closed off when new pipes are being laid or new buildings erected. Also, while we have tried to be as accurate and as current as possible with street and place names, city bureaucrats being what they are, these, too, will inevitably change as "politically incorrect" names are revamped. Our advice is to be flexible and to carry a current city map with you to supplement the ones in this book.

Many of these walks cover relatively long distances. Berlin is a huge city, as extensive as Greater London or New York, and noteworthy sites are not always concentrated along a short route. We highly recommend that you wear comfortable walking shoes and leave ample time for refreshments and cafe sitting. At times we mention museums or exhibits that you should see, but we have not included those stops in our time estimates. Particularly on Walk 1, we suggest you complete the walk, then return later to visit the excellent museums.

Inevitably, in a city as large and diverse as Berlin, it is difficult to include everything we think you should see in these four walks. We have therefore made additional suggestions in the Information and Advice section, and you'll find our selection of noteworthy museums in the final section of the book.

Information
and Advice

GETTING TO BERLIN

A valid passport is all that is required for most tourists visiting Germany; however, stays longer than ninety days require a visa. For tourist information in advance of your arrival, you can contact the German National Tourist Office, which has offices in New York (747 Third Avenue, 33rd Floor, New York, NY 10017; tel: 212-308-3300) and Los Angeles (444 South Flower Street, Suite 2230, Los Angeles, CA 90017; tel: 213-688-7332).

For assistance with hotel accommodations or general information on arrival in Berlin you can visit the tourist information office, *Verkehrsamt Berlin*, at Tegel Airport (open daily, 8 am to 11 pm), Bahnhof Zoologischer Garten (open Monday through Saturday, 8 am to 11 pm), the TV tower on Alexanderplatz (open daily, 8 am to 8 pm), or at the Europa Center (open Monday through Saturday, 8 am to 10:30 pm; Sunday 9 am to 9 pm).

By air

Flights to Berlin, whether direct from the States or via a connection, will most likely land at *Flughafen Berlin-Tegel*. Located in the former West Berlin, Tegel is a quick taxi ride (if the traffic cooperates) into central West Berlin. There is also a convenient bus (#109) that will take you to Bahnhof Zoologischer Garten. From there you can catch a connecting S-Bahn or U-Bahn (part of the inner-city rail network) or a bus or taxi to your hotel.

If your flight lands at *Flughafen Berlin-Tempelhof* (also in the west) or *Flughafen Berlin-Schönefeld* (in former East Berlin), you can take a U-Bahn or S-Bahn train into central East or West Berlin or take a taxi to your destination.

By train

Trains to Berlin often list their destination as the main train station, *Hauptbahnhof*. This station is located in what was formerly East Berlin and is unfortunately far from most of the hotels and tourist accommodations. If your train happens to stop en route at *Bahnhof Zoologischer Garten*, and many of them do, that is where we recommend you get out. Bahnhof Zoo, as it is often referred to, is the main train station in West Berlin. It is located at the end of Kurfürstendamm, and most of the tourist hotels are within a fifteen-minute walk of this station. There are major S-Bahn and U-Bahn stops at Zoo, many buses include Zoo on their routes, and taxis are plentiful. If you do arrive at the Hauptbahnhof, don't despair—the S-Bahn connects there and will quickly take you back to Zoo. Or you can catch a taxi.

GETTING AROUND BERLIN

Foreigners are quick to poke fun at the Germans' compulsion for schedules, but one rapidly learns to appreciate a touch of fanaticism when it comes to using Berlin's smooth and efficient public transportation system. In a city as sprawling as Berlin, it is a good idea to try to master the inner-city rail network, which includes an underground system (known as the U-Bahn) and an aboveground system (known as the S-Bahn). The two are connected and will get you just about anywhere you want to go. The double-decker buses are also efficient and convenient, and often coordinate with the rail network. Using bus and train together you can navigate the city with ease and sightsee along the way. With luck you may never have to rely on taxis, which of course are plentiful, reliable, not very expensive, and, at night, often faster than public transportation.

Some hints to help you get around easily: First, public transportation in Berlin is run by the *Berliner Verkehrs-Betriebe*, or BVG. You can pick up free maps and assorted schedules and buy special tickets from the main BVG information center just outside Bahnhof Zoologischer Garten at Hardenbergplatz (open daily, 8 am to 8 pm). In addition, you can often find BVG information agents in the main S-Bahn and U-Bahn stations, such as Wittenbergplatz, Zoologischer Garten, Friedrichstrasse, and Alexanderplatz; they have city maps and transportation schedules and can help direct you if you are lost or confused. We strongly encourage you to buy your own city map, however, and to pick up a free rail network map, which will be invaluable in planning your excursions and getting around town.

All train stations, including the more poorly marked ones in the former East Berlin, now have posted maps of the rail network and the unified city, and timetables should also be posted. If you can't find what you are looking for, don't hesitate to ask the person announcing the trains, who usually will try to solve your problem. Many bus stops, too, have posted maps, and all have route destinations and timetables; but with graffiti increasingly pervasive, they can sometimes be indecipherable.

Tickets

Tickets for the rail network and the buses (and streetcars in the East) are interchangeable and are good for two hours; each ticket costs 3.20 DM (about $2). You can also get several types of discounted tickets. If you are making a quick hop (six stops on the bus or three by rail), then you can use a *Kurzstreckenkarte*, which costs only 2.10 DM; if you are just traveling by bus along Kurfürstendamm between Wittenbergplatz and Rathenauplatz, then your ride will cost only 1.50 DM. A *Sammelkarte*, or multiple-ride ticket, allows you four rides for a slightly reduced price of 11 DM; a Sammelkarte for short-distance trips is also available for 6.70 DM. A twenty-four-hour pass is available for 12 DM and allows you an unlimited number of rides of unlimited duration. A six-day pass (good Monday through Saturday) is available for 32 DM, again giving you an unlimited number of trips. And finally, there is a one-week pass (which can be purchased only at the BVG office at Hardenbergplatz); it is good for a full seven days beginning when you purchase it and also costs 32 DM.

Purchase tickets on the bus, at rail station ticket counters, or at automatic vending machines located at every station. The machines take bills and coins and give change. Single-ride tickets and twenty-four and six-day passes do not need to be validated, but Sammelkarte do. Validate them using the yellow punch-in machine called an *Entwerter* located at entrances to rail platforms and behind the driver on buses; there is a section on the ticket for each ride. If you are transferring to the bus, you need only show your valid ticket to the driver.

Special routes

Several bus routes are of particular interest to tourists because they travel directly to and through major city attractions, most of which are in Berlin's Mitte district (see Walk 1). Try to sit up front on the top deck.

Bus #100, which leaves every ten minutes from Zoologischer Garten, makes a nice circuit through part of the Tiergarten, passes through the Brandenburger Tor, and heads up Unter den Linden past Alexanderplatz.

Bus #129 cuts a slightly different path, starting on the edge of Berlin's immense forest, the Grunewald, and traveling the length of Kurfürstendamm and along the banks of the Landwehrkanal past the Bauhaus Archiv and the Neue National Gallerie, a museum that houses an impressive collection of German Expressionist paintings. Farther on, the bus lets riders out at the Topography of Terror exhibit (corner of Wilhelmstrasse and Kochstrasse), and one stop more (Kochstrasse at Friedrichstrasse) puts visitors in front of the *Museumhaus am* Checkpoint Charlie and a block from the historic site itself. The line continues through Kreuzberg and ends at Hermannplatz in the middle-class neighborhood of Neukölln.

Bus #148 cuts a north-south passage from the Philharmonie, near Potsdamer Platz, to Zehlendorf, traveling up and down the main streets, Potsdamer Strasse and Schlossstrasse.

Rides on the S-Bahn, heading east from Zoologischer Garten, go through part of the Tiergarten and skirt historic sites in Berlin's Mitte district. Past Alexanderplatz the trains continue on through East Berlin neighborhoods that have not changed much since 1990 when the city became unified. The major difference is that new stores now line commercial streets where before there were far fewer selling fewer items. If you catch an S-Bahn going west, you will soon find yourself in the middle of neighborhoods with single-family homes (and villas) that border the Grunewald—the huge forest and lake district at the edge of the city that is a favorite weekend destination for Berliners from all walks of life.

Maps

Tourist maps of the city are available at many newspaper kiosks, at bookstores, and at tourist shops at the airports and major train stations. Two publishers have very good maps of Berlin that include a detailed map of the city center and the rail network: *Touristplan Berlin*, published by Falk, and *Stadtplan Berlin*, published by Kümmerly & Frey. Each map costs approximately 5 DM.

Bike rentals

Several companies rent bicycles, and some of the fancier hotels offer bikes to their guests. With red-paved bike routes lacing the city, it is not hard to get around this way. Pedestrians should beware of standing or walking in these red zones: Aggressive Berlin bikers are likely to run you down after a quick warning ring from their bell. One of the more interesting but unmarked bike routes navigates the former Berlin Wall border zone. In many places the asphalt is in bad repair, but the stretch of undeveloped land that winds through the city is tempting to explore. Unfortunately, the route is not continuous and there is no formal map or route, so you'll want to get a good city map and some advice before setting out. Bicycle rentals can be found at *Fahrradbüro*, Hauptstrasse 146 (Tel: 784 55 62), and at the Grunewald S-Bahn station (Tel: 811 58 29).

MONEY AND CURRENCY EXCHANGE

Germany functions as a cash society, which perhaps helps to explain the country's prosperity, but it also poses

Neue Wache

logistical difficulties for tourists used to putting everything on plastic. In general, major credit cards (Visa, Master-Card, and American Express) are accepted at most tourist shops and fancier restaurants and at hotels in all but the budget category. Once you get away from the bigger tourist haunts, however, cash is the medium of exchange. The currency throughout Germany and unified Berlin is the deutsche mark, which has been worth about $1.60.

You can change money at the newly opened American Express office (Uhlandstrasse 173, Monday through Friday, 9 am to 5:30 pm; Saturday, 9 am to 12 pm. Tel: 882 75 75) and at the currency exchange centers at Tegel Airport (open daily, 8 am to 10 pm) and Bahnhof Zoologischer Garten (Monday through Saturday, 7:30 am to 10 pm; Sunday, 8 am to 7 pm). Banks, too, will exchange currency; typical banking hours are 9 am to 12:30 pm with variable afternoon hours. You can also change money at less advantageous rates as a guest at most of the larger hotels.

CLIMATE AND CLOTHING

Berlin is noted for its fresh, clean air, *"die Berliner Luft,"* and its congenial continental climate. Nonetheless, keep in mind that Berlin is located in the far northeastern part of Germany, and the average temperatures reflect that reality. Daytime temperatures in summer rarely make it into the 80s, and evenings often cool down into the 60s, so being a tourist here is not a hot and exhausting venture. Spring and fall feature cooler temperatures: Daytime temperatures are often in the 40s or 50s, and evenings find the thermometer near freezing. However, even with these temperatures, when the sun shines, inveterate Berliners sip beer or coffee and eat ice cream at the sidewalk cafes that spring up throughout the city. Winter can be awfully grim here, with overcast gray skies, freezing temperatures, and ice-cold drizzle, but no matter the season, Berliners revel in the outdoors. As soon as the days are mild enough, tables and chairs fill the sidewalks in front of even the smallest cafes, and any weekend of the year finds locals strolling through the city's parks and around the several lakes that ring the city. Tourists, naturally enough, find it easy to adapt to this pace of life.

Residents of the city tend to dress in sensible, stylish clothing, but one wouldn't call them fashionable, like Parisians. Tourists can wear comfortable clothes for sightseeing during the day and not feel conspicuous or inappropriately underdressed. Comfortable shoes for walking long distances over cobblestoned surfaces are a necessity in this large city. There are no strict dress codes at most restaurants, and usually casual slacks with a dress shirt for men and a similar ensemble for women is sufficient. In the summer, a lightweight jacket or sweater for evenings might be needed since it can get cool.

HEALTH, MEDICAL EMERGENCIES, AND CONSULATES

Germany is a clean and efficient country, and there really aren't any health hazards, even in the more impoverished eastern portions of the country. While most Germans do not drink water from the tap, it is completely safe.

Should you require over-the-counter medicine or prescription drugs during your stay, you will need to locate an *Apotheke*, not a *Drogerie*. The latter sell toiletries while the former function as pharmacies. For after-hours emergencies, locate an apotheke and look on the door to find the address of the apotheke "on call," or you can call 1141 for the same information.

If a medical problem requires emergency care, you should call 112. The tourist information offices listed above have lists of English-speaking doctors and dentists. Should you need a hospital, you may have to pay a cash deposit up front.

Consulates

United States: Clayallee 170. Tel: 819 74 65
Great Britain: Uhlandstrasse 7–8. Tel: 309 52 92
Canada: Europa Center, 12th floor. Tel: 261 11 61

TELEPHONES, POST OFFICES, AND TOILETS

It used to be that if you were in East Berlin and needed a phone, you were better off heading back to the western part of the city to find one. Sadly, that is pretty much still the case. In the main tourist areas around Unter den Linden and Alexanderplatz, it is easier to find pay phones, but they are still not as plentiful as they are in the West.

Local calls cost 30 pfennigs (about 20 cents), but the hitch is to find a phone that takes coins since the city has converted many of the phones to the "convenient" phone card system. Phone cards can be purchased at the post office, but they cost 12 DM and 50 DM and aren't usually worth it except for the most phone-addicted tourists. However, they are a good way to make international calls without having to load the phone with coins. If you are desperate for a phone, head to the nearest post office (see below).

With reunification there has been a massive overhaul of the telephone system, and many numbers have changed as a result. An important number to know, therefore, is the one for information (01188). The area code for Berlin is 030.

A convenient branch of the post office can be found in Bahnhof Zoologischer Garten; it is open around the clock. Hours for other postal branches are Monday through Friday, 8 am to 6 pm; Saturday until noon. The post office symbol is a bugle, and it adorns bright yellow postal boxes that can be spotted throughout the city. All post offices have at least one pay phone; the phones may be coin operated, or you may have to request and pay for a phone line at the customer service counter.

Public toilets (or WCs) can be found at major train stations, such as Zoologischer Garten, Friedrichstrasse, and Alexanderplatz, and at some major tourist attractions, such as the Brandenburger Tor or Museumsinsel. However, the cost may be anywhere from 50 pfennigs to 1 DM at these locations. They are usually clean and have toilet paper, but it is always a good idea to have your own supply. Museums and most other similar tourist sites also have conveniently located free toilets that you shouldn't hesitate to use, and most restaurants will not object to your using their facilities.

FOOD AND DRINK

You probably did not choose Berlin for its cuisine. But what the city lacks in variety—only a few French, Asian, or Turkish establishments add a touch of spice to the hearty but mostly undistinguished German, Italian, and Greek restaurants—it makes up for in what the Germans call *Gemütlichkeit*; comfort and congeniality. You will find restaurants and cafes along almost every street of the city, and many of them place tables and chairs outside during mild weather; thus, dining out in Berlin can be a very pleasurable experience for the soul, if not tantalizing for the palate. At the back of the book we have included a number of neighborhood restaurants for those visitors who seek a particularly congenial evening. Especially when dining outside, sharing tables is not at all uncommon, but one should ask the occupants if they mind the company.

Long before dinner, however, the Germans enjoy languorous breakfasts, which are served well into the afternoon in dozens of cafes. Usually featuring a bit of alternative flair, these cafes are the places to read a newspaper, sip a *Milchkaffee*, and choose from a tasty assortment of breads and rolls (*Brötchen* or the Berlin specialty *Schrippen*) and cheeses and meats. You can round out the meal with yogurt or a soft-boiled egg (*Frühstücksei* or *gekochtes Ei*). Coffee in Germany is typically served by the cup (*Tasse*), with no refills, or by the pot (*Kännchen*), which gives you at least two cups, maybe more.

Lunch is the main meal for Germans, and restaurants often have an inexpensive *Tageskarte* (menu of the day) that includes soup and salad. Big salads are becoming easier to find. Turkish döner kebab stands and snack-stands (*Buden* or *Imbisses*), offering grilled or boiled sausages (*Rostbratwurst, Bockwurst,* and *Currywurst* are the most common), french fries (*Pommes frites*), hamburgers (*Bouletten*), and prepared salads, are the places for lighter stand-up meals. If you want to pack your own lunch, check out the food emporium on the sixth floor of *KaDeWe*, the premier

Marienkirche

department store at Wittenbergplatz. There you will find infinite varieties of breads, cheeses, cured meats, prepared salads, desserts, and on and on. There are also a dozen or so food counters, featuring German specialties as well as international cuisines, where you can sit and have a light meal.

Of course, all restaurants are open in the evening, and dinner is served from early evening until almost midnight. Pork, calves' *Schnitzel*, and potatoes (*Kartoffeln*) are the ubiquitous items on the menu, but you will also find

18

Königsberger Klopse, a north German meatball in a creamy caper sauce, grilled herring or *Bratherring*, and an array of tasty dumplings (*Klopse*) and noodles (*Spaetzle*). Seasonal specialties add a touch of variety. Look in particular for special *Spargel* menus, which feature tender white asparagus in the spring, and *Wild* menus, which offer game specialties such as venison, wild boar, and rabbit in the fall. If you are a vegetarian, beware: Soups and vegetables are usually prepared with pork.

Berliners take their beer very seriously. At the turn of the century, dozens of large breweries dotted the neighborhoods and entertained city people in huge outdoor beer gardens. These have all but disappeared, and the standard Berlin beers, *Kindl* and *Schultheiss*, are reliable but not great. A large variety of other German brews is available, however; we are particularly fond of *Radeberger* from Dresden and *Tegernsee* from Bavaria. The process of tapping beer is an artful and often time-consuming one; it can be a wait of five to ten minutes while the Biermeister forms a perfect head of foam on your draft beer. If you are very thirsty, you might want to order a big bottle such as *Weizenbier*, which is made from wheat; *krystal* is clear, while *hefe* is a bit darker. In the summer, try *Berliner Weisse*, beer with raspberry or woodruff syrup added; it is slightly sweet and very refreshing. There is no local wine, but all restaurants and cafes offer a more than satisfactory assortment.

Although a 15 percent service charge is included in your bill, it is common to round off the total. This is done in a straightforward fashion by announcing the rounded-off total before getting the change rather than by leaving coins behind on the table, a practice that may very well result in the waiter's scurrying into the street to return your change.

ADDITIONAL SITES

You might want to consider fitting in other attractions: a trip to Berlin's wonderful zoo, across from Bahnhof Zoologischer Garten, or an afternoon at the Botanischer Garten in Dahlem. The sprawling gardens here contain remarkable greenhouses, an immense variety of plants, plus ponds, meadows, and tranquil spots to sit and contemplate nature. Visitors can meander along winding paths that traverse "mountains" representing various countries and geographical regions from around the world.

Or you might take a subway trip out to one of several lakes that ring the city. Krumme Lanke, Schlachtensee, and Tegeler See are our favorite destinations. Boat trips along the Spree and Landwehrkanal or traversing the Havel and Wannsee are other good ways to obtain interesting views of the city, but the tours themselves are conducted in German. You can get information about the types of boat trips available from the BVG information office at Hardenbergplatz outside Bahnhof Zoologischer Garten. If you have time for a day trip outside Berlin, schedule an easy trip to Potsdam at the western edge of the city. Frederick the Great built the beautiful Schloss Sanssouci and its magnificent surrounding park as a summer retreat; a visit there will immediately reveal why it was named "without a care."

USEFUL WORDS AND PHRASES

hello	*hallo, guten Tag*
good-bye	*Auf Wiedersehen; Tschüss*
good morning	*guten Morgen*
good night	*gute Nacht*
please	*bitte*
thank you	*danke*
you're welcome	*bitte schön*
excuse me	*entschuldigen Sie mir; verzeihung*
yes	*ja*
no	*nein*

Do you speak English?	*Sprechen Sie Englisch?*
I don't speak German.	*Ich spreche nicht Deutsch.*
Can you help me?	*Können Sie mir helfen?*
Where is . . . ?	*Wo ist . . . ?*
I would like . . .	*Ich möchte . . .*
inexpensive	*billig*
to change money	*Geld wechseln*
traveler's checks	*Reiseschecks*
restaurant	*Restaurant, Gaststätte*
menu	*Speisekarte*
toilet	*Toilette, WC*
men	*Herren*
women	*Damen*
the check, please	*die Rechnung, bitte*
small change	*Kleingeld*
tip	*Trinkgeld*
entrance	*Eingang*
exit	*Ausgang*
train station	*Bahnhof*
bus or subway stop	*Haltestelle*
open	*offen*
closed	*geschlossen*
large	*gross*
small	*klein*

In the Restaurant

menu	*Speisekarte*
breakfast	*Frühstück*
lunch	*Mittagessen*
dinner	*Abendessen*
snack, small items	*kleine Gerichte*
drinks	*Getränke*

water	*Wasser*
wine	*Wein*
beer	*Bier*
tea	*Tee*
coffee	*Kaffee*
juice	*Saft*
rolls	*Brötchen, Schrippe*
soft-boiled egg	*gekochtes Ei*
fried eggs	*Spiegeleier*
scrambled eggs	*Rühreier*
appetizer	*Vorspeise*
soup	*Suppe*
main course	*Hauptgericht*
meat	*Fleisch*
ground beef	*Hackfleisch*
hamburger	*Boulette*
pork	*Schweinefleisch*
beef	*Rind*
veal	*Kalb*
lamb	*Lamm*
ham	*Schinken*
aspic	*Sülze*
poultry	*Geflügel*
chicken	*Huhn*
duck	*Ente*
game	*Wild*
breast	*Brust*
thigh	*Keule*
fish	*Fisch*
salmon	*Lachs*
herring	*Hering, Matjes*
sole	*Seezunge*
trout	*Forelle*
shrimp	*Garnelen*

vegetables	*Gemüse*
potatoes	*Kartoffeln*
french fries	*Pommes frites*
dumplings	*Knödeln*
noodles	*Nudeln, Spaetzle*
rice	*Reis*
carrots	*Mohrrüben*
asparagus	*Spargel*
mushrooms	*Champignons*
leek	*Lauch*
cabbage	*Sauerkraut, Rotkohl*
spices	*Gewürze*
sharp	*scharf*
mild	*mild*
salad	*Salat*
peppers	*Paprika*
cucumber	*Gurke*
fruit	*Frucht*
cheese	*Käse*
dessert	*Nachtisch*
cake	*Kuchen, Torte*
ice cream	*Eis*
baked	*gebacken*
roast	*gebraten*
steamed	*gedämpft*
smoked	*geräuchert*
pickled	*eingelegt*
stuffed	*gefüllt*

RECOMMENDED BOOKS

Perhaps the best introduction to the flavor of the city is Alfred Döblin's *Berlin Alexanderplatz*, an epic novel of Berlin in the 1920s that has been made into a movie. It is worth dipping into the book even if you don't read it all the way through. Christopher Isherwood's *Berlin Stories* conveys the mood of the city in the fateful years before the Nazi seizure of power. Thomas Wolfe has some powerful scenes of Berlin in the Third Reich in *You Can't Go Home Again*. More contemporary novels include Peter Schneider's wickedly funny *The Wall Jumper*.

More historical accounts of the city can be found in John Mander's *Berlin: The Eagle and the Bear*, Michael Simmons's *Berlin: The Dispossessed City*, Otto Friedrich's *Before the Deluge*, and Wolf von Eckardt and Sander L. Gilman's *Bertolt Brecht's Berlin: A Scrapbook of the Twenties*. Gordon Craig provides a marvelous introduction to Germany in general in *The Germans*. An excellent scholarly collection has been assembled by Charles W. Haxthausen and Heidrun Suhr: *Berlin: Culture and Metropolis*. Klaus Strohmeyer's *Berlin in Bewegung* is a notable two-volume scrapbook of Berlin impressions, letters, and documents.

HISTORY

If you unrolled a sixteenth-century map of Europe, you would not find Berlin. For hundreds of years it was little more than an undistinguished garrison city that served as the residence of the elector of Brandenburg and Prussia. Unlike Paris or London or Vienna, Berlin cannot boast of being founded by the Romans, nor was it a center of medieval learning or commerce. Paris, for example, already had a population of several hundred thousand when the first north German fishermen and merchants erected their wooden houses on the banks of the Spree River in the early thirteenth century. The warehouses, repair docks, and inns of the small island settlement of Cölln are mentioned for the first time in legal documents in 1237, a date that has since been regarded as the founding of Berlin. By the end of the fourteenth century a wooden bridge linked Cölln with thatched-roofed houses and fieldstone churches on the opposite, north shore, which was the village of Berlin.

Around the time that medieval records first mention Cölln, the Mongols were invading central Europe, and soon thereafter they crushed the combined armies of the Poles and Silesians and even occupied Breslau. But even more dangerous than invading armies was the lack of a stable political authority. Brandenburg changed hands frequently, and nominal rulers cared little for their far-off, exposed territory. Finally, in 1411, Friedrich von Hohenzollern, who had been appointed to protect and oversee Brandenburg, resolved to establish order in the territories. But in doing so he also extinguished the civic freedoms and tax-free rights of towns like Berlin and Cölln. The year 1443, when the Hohenzollerns built a fortress on the north end of Spree Island, marks the end of the independence of Berlin and the beginning of its role as a Hohenzollern residence.

The Hohenzollerns ranked low among European rulers. Although they inherited territories in Prussia to add to those in Brandenburg, the family had few cultural pretensions; besides, they were merely electors, appointed to their post by the Holy Roman Emperor. It was only in 1701 that the emperor recognized the Hohenzollerns as kings. As a result, their residence did little to favor Berlin and Cölln. What the towns gained in military protection they more than lost in commercial and political independence. The fortunes of Berlin turned from bad to worse in the religious wars of the seventeenth century. During the rampages of the Thirty

Years' War (1618–48), Berlin was forced to endure military occupations and pay onerous financial tributes. After a generation of war and impoverishment, Berlin and Cölln were devastated. The Hohenzollerns, who had fled to fortresses in East Prussia, returned to Berlin in March 1643 to find that only the poorer half of the population remained. In Berlin, more than 300 of the 845 houses stood empty, and almost every other house in Cölln had been abandoned as well.

It would not have been surprising if the wasted Spree settlements had disappeared completely. During the Thirty Years' War, hundreds of towns throughout Central Europe were abandoned to the forests, with only fieldstones and sunken foundations remaining to mark the vanished places. The Hohenzollerns resolved to rebuild their small state, however, regenerating commerce and establishing a strong garrison. In the 150 years that followed, Berlin emerged as a completely redone and fairly prosperous capital, but it did so due to the militarization of Prussian politics. A strong state required a strong army, and then as now, a strong army needed a prosperous tax base; thus Friedrich Wilhelm (ruled 1640–88), the so-called Great Elector, went about rehabilitating Berlin's commerce. He garrisoned thousands of soldiers in the town, built new districts south of the Spree, and invited Protestant Huguenot exiles from France as well as Jewish refugees from Austria to become residents. And while he gave capital-rich foreigners tax privileges, he also imposed numerous financial burdens on ordinary townspeople. Berlin was thus run largely to create revenues for the Prussian armies. The straight-edged streets of Friedrichstadt (Walk 1), the groomed parade grounds along the city's edge, and the newly erected excise wall all attested to the strong military aspect of Berlin. Later in the eighteenth century, the "Enlightened Despot," King Frederick the Great (ruled 1740–86), added cultural institutions such as intellectual academies, theaters, and the opera, making the new Berlin a model city of European absolutism.

Thanks to the spartan regimes of the Hohenzollerns, by 1800, Prussia boasted the fourth largest army in Europe even though it ranked only thirteenth among the states in population.

Nothing changed the face of Berlin more than the onset of the Industrial Revolution. After the Napoleonic Wars (1805–13), as after the Thirty Years' War, Prussian officials restored military power by economic means. Berlin quickly became a center of technical education and economic liberalism; transplanted English engineers now played the part that émigré French Huguenots had a century earlier. Just outside the city walls, entrepreneurs set up their metalworking and textile factories and attracted thousands of immigrants from the impoverished rural countryside. In just a few decades, Berlin acquired a large proletarian population. Canals and railways gradually linked Berlin with the rest of Germany, making it a vital commercial and industrial center. At the same time, Berlin increasingly became a city of densely populated five-storey tenements, which added new social problems and political tensions. By the late 1840s, soaring food costs and poor working conditions as well as the persistently reactionary politics around the Hohenzollern court set the stage for the Revolution of 1848.

The political struggle for constitutional rights and liberties failed in 1848 as it had in 1813, but it would be a mistake to overlook the freedoms that metropolitan Berliners did come to enjoy. Industrialization, more than anything else, created a diverse and colorful working class that no amount of regulation by the court or the police could completely control. Diverse groups of Silesians, Saxons, Poles, and Jews streamed into the metropolis, went to work in factories, and established businesses of their own. At the same time, socialists gained political strength, organizing trade unions and creating a dense network of social associations, bicycle clubs, choirs, and funeral societies.

The unification of Germany under the leadership of

Prussia in 1871 and the designation of Berlin as the new imperial capital, with Wilhelm I crowned kaiser of the German Empire, only hastened the transformation of the once provincial Hohenzollern residence into a thriving industrial metropolis. In the thirty years preceding World War I, Greater Berlin doubled, from two to four million inhabitants. Although the towns and villages that surrounded Berlin—Köpenick, Spandau, Schöneberg, Steglitz, Charlottenburg—had long since merged with the growing city, they retained administrative independence until their incorporation in 1920.

On the eve of World War I, Berlin lived a double life. On the one hand, there was the large portion of the population that voted socialist, drank beer in the gardens of Bötzow's brewery, and took their Sundays in the forests and lakes of the Grunewald. And on the other hand, there were the Berliners who paraded to brass bands, cheered the kaiser, and veiled the city in pompous imperial façades and commemorative statuary. For a time, in the heady patriotic atmosphere of the beginning of the war in 1914, these two groups seemed to merge. But the absence of basic political rights, the increasingly desperate economic hardships of the war, and the futility of Germany's war aims eventually pitted ordinary Berliners against the monarchy. In November 1918, amid street demonstrations and revolutionary strikes, Wilhelm II abdicated and Social Democrats declared Germany's first democratic government, the Weimar Republic. Unfortunately, harsh economics and unfulfilled political expectations kept Berliners divided. As democrats battled monarchists, socialists battled Communists, and the Nazis clashed with all parties, the Weimar Republic had little chance for political stability or longevity.

The streets of Berlin in the 1920s were not simply a dangerous political battleground. The ruinous inflation in 1922–23 and the credit squeeze that followed left the city looking more and more physically forlorn. Cheap bars, brothels, and cabarets prospered in this gambler's economy. In the tiny one-room and two-room apartments that constituted most of Berlin's households lived the impoverished pensioners who had lost their life savings, clerks who frantically tried to hold on to their jobs, and workers who suffered again and again the seasonal swings of unemployment.

But the end of the war and the downfall of the monarchy also released enormous intellectual energy. Writers such as Bertolt Brecht and Alfred Döblin, painters such as Otto Dix and George Grosz, and architects such as Walter Gropius and Mies van der Rohe made Berlin the capital of twentieth-century cultural life. There was a breathless sense of excitement about the city, that the unforgiving economics and uncertain politics of the 1920s only enhanced. Visitors frequently compared the hectic rhythm of Berlin with life on the edge of a volcano. The onset of the Great Depression brought Berliners up short, however. With two out of every five workers unemployed in 1932, excitement shifted to panic, and the political fortunes of the Nazis took off.

Although Berlin was never a Nazi stronghold, the National Socialists did respectably well in the city. After Hitler's accession to power on January 30, 1933, the marks of the free-wheeling Berlin of the 1920s were gradually erased in any case. Hitler conceived Berlin as the grand capital of his Germanic empire and set about erecting monumental government buildings and sweeping boulevards. Only the onset of World War II in September 1939 kept Hitler and his architect Albert Speer from totally revamping the central districts of Berlin. Far more successful was the Nazi attempt to "Aryanize" the population of Berlin. Berlin had long been the center of Jewish life in Germany, but after the National Socialists came to power, they squeezed German Jews out of public life and eventually forcibly segregated them from the rest of German society. After 1933, two out of every three Berlin Jews quit the city. Between 1942 and 1945, the Nazis deported and murdered the rest. The ethnic and cultural diversity that the Nazis feared so intensely has only slowly returned to present-day Berlin.

The horrors of World War II approached Berlin after 1943 when Allied air raids laid waste to the old core of the city, an ironic fulfillment of Hitler's ambition to level old Berlin in order to erect a new Rome. By the end of the war, in May 1945, almost two million people had abandoned the capital, and half the buildings had been destroyed or damaged. The very future of the city seemed in doubt. But its apparent physical destruction obscured the degree to which factory machinery and vital aspects of the city's infrastructure had survived the war. Quickly, well-established market and rail networks recovered, and the city's commerce revived. What is more, the thousands of inhabitants who had remained or returned to Berlin cleared the rubble, refounded newspapers, theater companies, and political parties, and tried to recapture the years that had been lost to the repressive Third Reich. This sense of resilience eventually earned Berliners considerable admiration around the world.

The victorious Allies never intended to divide Germany or the former capital. Indeed, a prosperous Germany would help defray the costs of occupation. However, growing tensions between the world's two postwar superpowers, the United States and the Soviet Union, disassembled plans for European economic reconstruction and led to the gradual separation of the zone occupied by the Soviets. Allied differences over currency reform prompted the yearlong Soviet blockade of western Berlin and finally ended in the 1949 establishment of two separate German states. But the future of Berlin itself remained uncertain. Although the city was nestled deep within the Soviet zone, it was divided into Allied sectors

Marx and Engels

and occupied by French, British, American, and Soviet forces. At the same time, the former capital remained a functioning metropolis; commuters and streetcars crossed sector boundaries at will.

Borders became clear-cut and all ambiguities vanished, however, in the early morning of August 13,

1961, when East German soldiers erected the Berlin Wall, effectively locking their fellow citizens inside the Soviet bloc. For more than twenty-eight years Berliners lived in two separate cities with two different futures. Each side grew increasingly estranged from the other. The division of the city may have seemed unnatural at first, but it eventually became a rather natural condition, so much so that when the wall fell in November 1989, it caught even expert Berlin watchers by surprise.

When Soviet leader Mikhail Gorbachev came to power in 1985, he inaugurated a period of liberalization that effectively created a half-dozen avenues to reform and reaction in East Europe. While Poland, Hungary, and even Czechoslovakia gradually reinstituted political and economic liberties, the East German regime tightened its grip. This created an intolerable situation for East Germans, who while frustrated by political developments at home remained free to travel to other Eastern bloc countries. By the autumn of 1989, thousands of East Germans had fled to Hungary and then Czechoslovakia, a massive statement of protest that was replayed in the streets of Leipzig and Berlin. Huge demonstrations in October and November 1989 first generated promises of political reform, then simply accelerated the confusion prevailing in East Berlin, and finally led to the uncertain statement on November 9 that East Germans were free to travel where they wished. By evening the Berlin Wall had fallen; a few weeks later the East German regime lost all political authority.

Unfortunately, the ebullience that greeted the city's reunification in 1990 has yet to overcome the differences and resentments that continue to divide East and West Berliners. The manner in which Bonn managed reunification and the way in which speculators took advantage of East Germans afterward continue to grate. Yet it is just these frictions that make the city so interesting and exciting. The future of Berlin is by no means exhausted by its new role as the capital of a reunified Germany; recent history has cast all sorts of contentious political and intellectual figures who will shape and reshape the city's history for decades to come.

Walk · 1

Berlin Mitte

THE HISTORIC CITY CENTER

Reichstag

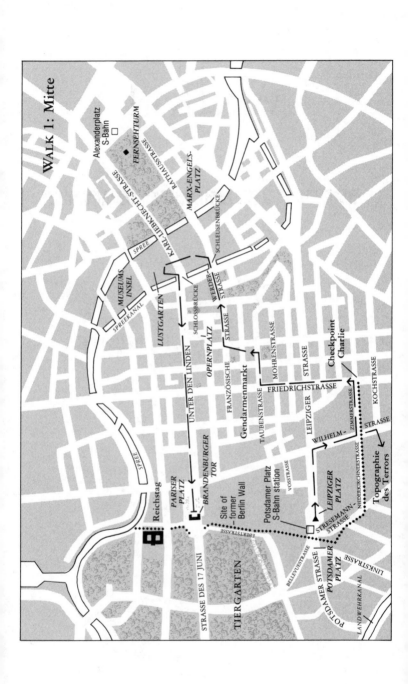

WALK 1: Mitte

Alexanderplatz S-Bahn

FERNSEHTURM

RATHAUSSTRASSE

KARL-LIEBKNECHT-STRASSE

MARX-ENGELS-PLATZ

SCHLEUSENBRÜCKE

SPREE

MUSEUMS INSEL

SPREEKANAL

LUSTGARTEN

WERDER-STRASSE

SCHLOSSBRÜCKE

OPERNPLATZ

STRASSE

MOHRENSTRASSE

UNTER DEN LINDEN

FRANZÖSISCHE

Gendarmenmarkt

STRASSE

Checkpoint Charlie

TAUBENSTRASSE

FRIEDRICHSTRASSE

KOCHSTRASSE

LEIPZIGER

STRASSE

PARISER PLATZ

BRANDENBURGER TOR

Site of former Berlin Wall

WILHELM-

ZIMMERSTRASSE

Reichstag

VOSSTRASSE

Potsdamer Platz S-Bahn station

LEIPZIGER PLATZ

NIEDERKIRCHNERSTRASSE

Topographie des Terrors

STRASSE DES 17 JUNI

EBERTSTRASSE

STRESEMANN-STRASSE

SPREE

BELLEVUESTRASSE

POTSDAMER PLATZ

NIEDERKIRCHNERSTRASSE

TIERGARTEN

POTSDAMER STRASSE

LINKSTRASSE

LANDWEHRKANAL

Starting Point: Potsdamer Platz
Transportation: S-Bahn lines 1 and 2, or U-Bahn line 2, to Potsdamer Platz
Length: About 3 hours

This walk, like the other three, is best taken during business hours when shops are open and streets crowded, but it also works rather well on weekends.

Berlin's *Mitte* district, or midtown, encompasses what remains of the medieval settlements of Berlin and Cölln on either side of the Spree River; of the heart of the capital of Prussia in the eighteenth-century Age of Absolutism; of the bustling commercial center of Berlin at the end of the nineteenth century; of the seat of government throughout the centuries up to the Nazi period; and, finally, of the pulse point of the Cold War. This long walk begins at Potsdamer Platz—the former hub of the imperial capital but now an empty space—and loops around to the Brandenburger Tor, the scene of military triumph, defeat, and anarchy. Along the way we will visit some of

Berlin's most famous sites and cover the city's evolution from a devastated town of some six thousand souls at the end of the Thirty Years' War (1648) to its emergence as one of the most industrially advanced and densely populated cities in Europe three centuries later.

The story of Berlin is the story of constant change. The jarring transformations that have shaped the city can best be appreciated by arriving at Potsdamer Platz by way of the underground S-Bahn. Even at the cost of a detour, it is worth taking S-Bahn line 1 or 2 to Potsdamer Platz to ascend the stairs of the once abandoned station and emerge onto what used to be the busiest square in all Berlin. In the S-Bahn station, follow the signs to Vossstrasse. (U-Bahn line 2 also serves Potsdamer Platz.) As you emerge onto Potsdamer Platz, the Brandenburger Tor is clearly visible about 500 yards ahead of you. Hitler's mammoth Reich Chancellory building once stood on the opposite side of Vossstrasse; all that remains now is an empty lot. Turn around and walk toward the busy traffic on Leipziger Strasse. You are just inside what was once East Berlin; the wall followed Ebertstrasse on your right. At Leipziger Strasse, you are at the historic big-city intersection of **Potsdamer Platz**.

Potsdamer Platz, a desolate, windswept expanse of broken asphalt mixed with the mud and sand that underlies the entire city, is now being invaded by trailers and cranes marking massive construction sites. Despite the absence of permanent landmarks and buildings, traffic is jammed for hundreds of yards since this natural throughway connects the eastern and western halves of the city. But scattered around you are traces of German history, composing an archeological record of deeds and misdeeds from the time of old Prussia to the recent Communist past.

Potsdamer Platz was on the very edge of eighteenth-century Berlin. Beyond it lay the *Tiergarten*, the former deer park of the Prussian kings, and the road to Potsdam. Until 1869 the city's toll wall, which replaced the old

BERLINER VERKEHR:
Potsdamerplatz und
Blick in die Leipzigerstr

Potsdamer Platz in the 1920s

medieval fortifications, ran along the edge of the park connecting Potsdamer Tor to the Brandenburger Tor and thirteen other gates. It kept duty-free goods out of the city and Prussia's sad-faced conscripts in. Over the course of the nineteenth century, wealthy merchants, nobles, and officers built their villas just outside the city gates, along the shady boulevards that bordered the Tiergarten. In time, Potsdamer Platz became known as the elegant "West End" of Berlin.

Industrial development, however, quickly changed the character of the district. An immense railway station was built near the platz in the 1840s (almost 180 degrees opposite the Brandenburger Tor), and new urban development rapidly encroached upon the quiet villas at the edge of the park. Potsdamer Platz became the busy intersection that connected the city's eastern core with its western frontier. By the end of the nineteenth century, grand hotels, department stores, movie theaters, and office buildings made Potsdamer Platz the "Times Square" of Berlin.

The glory days of Potsdamer Platz are hard to imagine looking at this wasteland. There is no hint of the huge hotels and noisy restaurants that once stood here, each lit with beckoning neon signs and crowded with pleasure seekers. With hundreds of streetcars and automobiles passing every hour, this intersection was so busy that Europe's first streetlight was erected on Potsdamer Platz in 1924. Today, the traffic has returned, but only two buildings have survived to witness the square's renewal: To your right (as you stand at the intersection of Ebert and Leipziger Strasse, with Vossstrasse behind you), just in from the corner of Bellevuestrasse, you see a wing of the **Grand Hotel Esplanade**, built in 1908; and farther ahead, on the right, on the dead-end Potsdamer Strasse, is the wine restaurant **Huth**, once known for its fine claret but identifiable now only by its distinctive corner cupola.

The rest of the very metropolitan Potsdamer Platz is gone. Gone is Cafe Josty, which stood just in front of the Hotel Esplanade on the broad corner of Potsdamer and Bellevuestrasse. From the garden tables of Josty, patrons could watch the tumult of big-city traffic or read the scandalous headlines of the afternoon papers. Across Bellevuestrasse from Josty (to the right, looking at Hotel Esplanade) stood the Grand Hotel Bellevue, which in the late 1920s made way for the ultramodern Columbus House, designed by Erich Mendelssohn. Moving clockwise, the ritzy Palast Hotel dominated the corner you are standing on. And across Leipziger Strasse reigned Hotel Fürstenhof. Gone also is the well-lit façade of Haus Vaterland, an amusement palace that opened its doors in 1928. Advertising "the world in one house," Haus Vaterland could accommodate eight thousand guests in its movie theater, gigantic cafe, and numerous theme bars, which included a Turkish coffeehouse, a Spanish bodega, an American "Wild West" bar, and a Rhineland wine terrace that was swept by a mechanical thunderstorm every half-hour. Haus Vaterland was nothing if not adaptable: When the Allies faced off against the Axis powers in World War II, the American bar was dismantled and more "politically correct" Italian and Japanese attractions were offered in its place.

The most famous building near the square was Wertheim's, Germany's most opulent department store, built by Alfred Messel in 1897–1904. Its imposing granite pillars and glass windows stretched nearly 900 feet along the north side of Leipziger Strasse (on the left side of the street as you look toward the television tower)—as far as the massive Air Ministry, a wing of which can be seen at the end of the block on the right. According to the journalist Leo Colze, shoppers moved through a labyrinth of stock-filled showrooms that "narrow into small passageways and long corridors, then open onto broad squares, form cozy corners and nooks, and end in special salons and rooms that are closed to the public." Wertheim was a magical city within a city, and its Christmas windows were known to children throughout Berlin. The store was appropriated from its Jewish owners by the Nazis in 1938, heavily damaged in World War II, set afire by East German workers protesting increased work quotas in the uprising on June 17, 1953, and subsequently razed entirely. The property has been returned to the Wertheim Corporation, which is planning to rebuild on the site. In the meantime, a discotheque, Tresor, has opened in Wertheim's rediscovered old basement safes.

Parallel to the axis between Potsdamer Platz and the Brandenburger Tor, on the other side of the new apartment buildings on the right, is **Wilhelmstrasse**, a street that had been lined with ministerial palaces and became synonymous with German diplomacy after unification in 1871. (Please note: Wilhelmstrasse was renamed Otto-Grotewohl-Strasse by the East Germans and was changed once again to Toleranz Strasse in the last months before reunification; West Berlin continued to designate the street by its old name, and it is not clear what it will be called in the future.) The Foreign Office, for example, was located at Wilhelmstrasse 75–76, about halfway toward the gate. It was here that so many of the crises leading up to World War I were played out: Kaiser Wilhelm II's colonial struggles with France, the naval arms race with England, and the assassination of Archduke Francis Ferdinand in Sarajevo in June 1914. The gardens of the Chancellory, Wilhelmstrasse 77, extended into this area as well. In fact, much of the open area between the gate and Leipziger Strasse were gardens behind the ministries and residences. Bismarck lived at the Chancellory until 1890, and Hitler moved in on January 30, 1933, cheered by thousands of his brownshirted supporters who marched down Wilhelmstrasse in a torchlight parade. Just around the corner, on Leipziger Strasse, a prewar sightseer would also have found (on the left) the headquarters of the Navy and (on the right) the War Office. These buildings are all gone now, of course.

Potsdamer Platz also reveals traces of *Germania*, the "thousand-year imperial city" that Hitler hoped Berlin would become in the Third Reich. In the late 1930s, Hitler and his architect Albert Speer envisioned a triumphal north-south boulevard that would have swept right through this square, past the Reichstag, and toward a colossal assembly hall that was to have been larger than Saint Peter's in Rome and would seat as many as 150,000 patriots. As the Allies flattened more and more acres in central Berlin, Hitler laconically observed that now Germania was closer to realization than ever. Although Germania was never built, the former Air Ministry, which still stands on Wilhelmstrasse with its northern wing on Leipziger Strasse (built in 1934–36), anticipated the monumental scale the new city would assume. And the little mound of earth in the foreground on the right as you look toward the Brandenburger Tor marks the location of Hitler's newly built Chancellory (completed in 1939 but blown up by the Soviets in 1945) and the underground bunker where the dictator spent the last weeks of World War II before his suicide. How long this unmarked site will remain here is anyone's guess.

The real record of Hitler's work, however, is not any particular structure but simply the desolation around you. After all, Hitler's war invited the Allied bombers that gutted the inner city. And it was because of World War II that eastern Germany was occupied by the Soviets and Berlin was divided in half. The boundaries between the Soviet and American sectors and, after August 1961, the Berlin Wall ran right through Potsdamer Platz and between the Brandenburger Tor and the Reichstag; its course followed very closely the old city wall that had stood a century earlier. West Berlin prospered on the left; East Berlin crumbled on the right.

The Berlin Wall finally destroyed Potsdamer Platz, creating a borderland out of a central square. Wartime ruins were cleared or neglected rather than reconstructed. The streetcars that had clogged the boulevards before the war no longer crossed from east to west after the mid-1950s. Pedestrian traffic became more difficult as well. For West Berliners, the city center moved to the Kurfürstendamm; in the East, the center shifted to Alexanderplatz, where the television tower served to symbolize the socialist new start. By the early 1980s, Potsdamer Platz resembled a no-man's-land churned up by barrages of history. Trees and bushes flourished between the streetcar tracks and along the crumbling curbs. Nature lovers even reported migratory birds that had not been seen in Berlin for decades. In her poem "Naturschutzgebiet" (Nature Preserve), Sarah Kirsch described this abandoned place:

> *Die weltstädtischen Kaninchen*
> *Hüpfen sich aus auf dem Potsdamer Platz*
> *Wie soll ich angesichts dieser Wiesen*
> *Glauben, was mir mein Grossvater sagte*
> *Hier war der Nabel der Welt*
> *Als er in jungen Jahren mit seinem Adler*
> *Ein schönes Mädchen chauffierte.*

Durch das verschwundene Hotel
Fliegen die Mauersegler
Die Nebel steigen
Aus wunderbaren Wiesen und Sträuchern
Kaum sperrt man den Menschen den Zugang
Tut die Natur das ihre durchwächst
Noch das Pflaster die Strassenbahnschienen.

Metropolitan rabbits
Hop to their delight on Potsdamer Platz
Looking at this meadow
How can I believe what my grandfather recounted
Here was the very center of the world
When he was a young man in his Adler
driving a beautiful young girl.

Through the walls of the vanished hotel
The black martins sail
Fog rises
From fantastic fields and bushes
People have barely shut the gateway
And nature makes sure it creeps
among cobblestones between streetcar tracks.*

The future of Potsdamer Platz is uncertain. To the south of Leipziger Strasse, around the wine restaurant Huth, Daimler-Benz and Sony are building huge corporate complexes. The traffic that has rediscovered the geographical center of the reunified city will probably be diverted into an underground tunnel. Wertheim has also expressed the intention of returning to its old location on Leipziger Strasse. But the showy boulevards, the cafes, and the eighteenth-century palaces and ministries on Wilhelmstrasse are gone forever. Even the Berlin Wall has dis-

*From Sarah Kirsch's poem, 'Naturschutzgebiet,"
in Erdreich (Stuttgart: Deutsche Verlag-Anstalt,
1982), p. 48.

44

East German mural on the former Air Ministry Building

appeared without a trace. It would be a shame if this empty expanse leading to the Brandenburger Tor—a place that marks so well the ruins of German history—were allowed to simply disappear or be remodeled so that its power to evoke the haunted past of the city was lost.

We'll leave Potsdamer Platz now by walking toward the TV tower on the left-hand side of Leipziger Strasse. You will pass the eight-sided outline of Leipziger Platz, an eighteenth-century parade ground that lay just inside when Potsdamer Platz was situated just outside the old city gates. A few steps farther and, fifty years ago, you would have walked past Wertheim's and, on the opposite side, the Prussian Landtag. At Wilhelmstrasse (which may be marked Toleranz or Otto-Grotewohl-Strasse), turn right and cross the street at the light. Straight ahead is the former **Air Ministry.** Completed in 1935, this massive structure was built in a spare, streamlined style that is not usually associated with Nazi architects. Like Hermann Goering's *Luftwaffe* (Air Force), the building symbolized the modern and technologically adept side of National Socialism. It is also something of a paradox that the offices of the Luftwaffe survived the aerial bombardment of Berlin nearly intact. After the war, it served the East German government as an all-purpose office building. (A patriotic 1952 mural glorifying the socialist project is still visible on the Leipziger Strasse side.) Today, it is the headquarters of the *Treuhand*, the powerful office charged with restructuring commerce and industry in former East Germany. Since the Treuhand has closed down hundreds of businesses and thereby added to East German unemployment, the building retains a sinister aspect for many Berliners. It is slated to become the Ministry of Economics when the German government moves to Berlin.

After a long block and a half (past the intersection of Niederkirchner and Zimmerstrasse, where a section of the wall still stands), you can enter the grounds of the former administrative headquarters of the *Gestapo*, the secret state police in the Third Reich, opposite Kochstrasse. At this site the crimes of Hitler are remembered in a stunning exhibition, **Topographie des Terrors** (Topography of Terror), which describes not only the atrocities committed by Berlin's Gestapo but also the history of the surrounding streets. Like Potsdamer Platz, these grounds were once along the edge of Berlin where aristocrats built their summer residences, including the 1739 palace that was later named after nineteenth-century resident Prince Albrecht of Prussia. The palace stood right at the Wilhelmstrasse exhibit entrance, and much of the open space here used to be gardens. Over the course of the nineteenth century, however, the tumultuous growth of the industrial city encroached on this gracious living. By 1900 imposing museums and hotels and the Prussian Diet surrounded the two-storey palace. All that has survived is the newly redone Prussian Landtag (which will house Berlin's city parliament) and the **Martin-Gropius-Bau**, the ornate building ahead of you, completed in 1881 by the father of the famous Bauhaus architect Walter Gropius and now a museum housing multiple exhibits. After 1933, the Nazis rented many of the buildings along Prinz-Albrecht (now Niederkirchner) and Wilhelmstrasse, including the (vanished) palace, and set up their Gestapo headquarters. You will also want to tour the grounds, which are dotted with well-marked German and English signs that give a better sense of prewar Berlin (the maps are very helpful in getting your bearings).

The Gestapo complex was the most feared location in all Berlin. It was here, in a former industrial arts school and adjacent hotel, the Prinz-Albrecht, that Himmler, Heydrich, and Kaltenbrunner had their offices. In the basement, which has been partially excavated and serves as the Topography of Terror exhibition gallery, hundreds of political opponents of the Nazis were interrogated, tortured, or killed. Among the prisoners was Erich Honecker, a young Communist resistance fighter who was first arrested on December 4, 1935. He was better known later as general secretary of the East German Communist Party. Many of the conspirators in the assassination plot against Hitler on July 20, 1944, were also first brought here. These blocks were heavily bombed in the final months of the war, and among the ruins a passerby later found a scrap of paper with the last words of Harro Schulze-Boysen, who had been executed in 1942 as a leader of the resistance group Rote Kapelle, or Red Orchestra. He wrote: *"Die letzten Argumente/Sind Strang und Fallbeil nicht. Und unsre heutigen Richter sind/Noch nicht das Weltgericht."* (Nooses and guillotines are not final arguments. And today's judges are not the final court of justice.) After the war, the grounds were allowed to deteriorate. Until its designation as a historical memorial in 1987, this block had been leveled to make way for a parking lot, a practice ground for new drivers, and a rubble pit.

An excellent English-language guide to the exhibit is available. You might want to save Topography of Terror for another day, but if you want to enter, step through

The Berlin Wall

the revolving gate and head toward the red-brick Martin-Gropius-Bau. The historical exhibit is housed in the low-slung white building straight ahead.

Exit the exhibition by returning to Wilhelmstrasse; turn left and then right onto Zimmerstrasse. Along this street, which follows the route of the **Berlin Wall**, you can see how the wall tore through the city, leaving gaping holes, empty spaces, and bricked-up windows. The fine red-brick building on the left at #86–91 was **Concert House Clou**, a cavernous theater in which Adolf Hitler made his Berlin debut in 1927 and in which Berlin Jews were rounded up before being sent to Auschwitz in 1943. After one block, turn left, and you come to **Checkpoint Charlie**, flashpoint of the Cold War. The border-crossing area covered the huge expanse to your right (as you look up Friedrichstrasse), although the complex has been largely dismantled. Tourists and tour buses still stop here, attracted by a wall that no longer stands, and street merchants, attracted by the tourists, continue to turn over surplus East German goods. A few slabs of concrete and remnants of the "death strip" have been retrieved and put on display, but they do not summon up the Cold War atmosphere of the place. Before 1989, harsh electric lights bathed the entire complex in an eerie glow, posted signs warned idle sightseers not to cross too far, and Allied soldiers suspiciously eyed their East German counterparts. Checkpoint Charlie seemed to be a set left over from an old Cold War movie. In fact, American and Soviet tanks faced each other here in the fall of 1961. In the years before détente, many people feared that the superpowers would stumble into a world war over the issue of Berlin, which Nikita Khrushchev once described as "the testicles of the West. When I want the West to scream, I squeeze on Berlin."

Ultimately, however, the Berlin Wall probably defused rather than exacerbated superpower tensions. Once the wall went up in 1961, East Germany dropped its claims on West Berlin. For the socialist German Democratic Republic, the existence of the capitalist island of West Berlin in the middle of its territory was an affront to national sovereignty. Prior to the construction of the wall, after all, East and West Berliners could move about the city with relative ease. People living in the East held jobs in the West, visited family and friends, and spent evenings at Western (that is, capitalist) movies, theaters, and restaurants. The permeable border also meant that thousands of skilled workers and scientists could flee East Germany each month simply by walking across Potsdamer Platz or taking the subway into West Berlin. When East Germany, supported by the Soviet Union, advanced claims on the entire city in 1958, the Berlin crisis flared. Although the United States opposed any change in the status of Berlin, it was not at all clear whether it would risk nuclear war.

In the meantime, the crisis quickened the flow of refugees into West Berlin. Five thousand a week were registered in June 1961. In the early hours of Sunday morning, August 13, after the last moviegoers had returned home from Western theaters, the East Germans finally acted. Along the 103 miles around West Berlin they stretched barbed wire (bought from an English company) and began to erect their "anti-fascist protective wall." The wall's extraordinarily hard concrete, which turned out to be one of the best products ever manufactured in Berlin, effectively plugged the brain drain. At the same time it indicated that East Germany had dropped its claims to West Berlin, an "island" of capitalism in the socialist sea. For the next twenty-eight years the western side of the city was simply left blank on maps published by the East German state.

The wall ended the Berlin crisis but deepened the Berlin tragedy. Families were now divided, unable to communicate or visit. Following the borders of city boroughs, the wall ran right through the middle of neighborhood streets. It took years of patient negotiations before agreements on telephone calls and West Berlin visitation rights were reached. Every year East Berliners made daredevil escapes, which are recounted in the excellent **Museum Haus am Checkpoint Charlie** (half a block down Friedrichstrasse; open daily from 9 am to 10 pm). Unfortunately, the great majority of escapees were either caught or killed by border guards. On August 17, 1962, two blocks from Checkpoint Charlie, eighteen-year-old Peter Fechter slowly bled to death just a few feet from the border, in full view of despairing West Berliners. A helpless rage indicted both the American military police, which stood by, unwilling to violate the border, and East German officials, who carelessly picked up Fechter's lifeless body behind a tear-gas smoke screen fifty-eight minutes later. Nonetheless, the two halves of the "Siamese City" grew apart. Each side had its own airport, television tower, zoo, and postal museum. Newcomers from the eastern state of Saxony crowded into East Berlin, while longtime residents slowly abandoned the isolated city that West Berlin had become, making room for students, artists, and foreign workers. As a result, when the wall finally did come down in November 1989, Berliners were generally strangers to one another.

Checkpoint Charlie

What made Checkpoint Charlie so fascinating until 1989 was not so much the wall itself but the fact that Western tourists could pass between the two cities. The passage up Friedrichstrasse to the border complex was always something of an adventure. In a recent article in *American Scholar*, Ruth Gay, a historian of Jews in Germany and a frequent visitor to the city, remembers: "The visitor was sluiced through a series of dingy rooms, the windows hung with the inevitable lace curtains of East German bureaucracy. But no signs were posted; there was no indication of what was expected or of how to accomplish the transition from West to East. Applicants quickly learned, like newly arrived prisoners, by close observation and without talking, how to get forms, where to surrender that precious Western passport and wait for its return, where to make the obligatory exchange of money at the outrageous rate of one East mark to one West. All under the basilisk stares of teenaged guards, male and female, who breathed the fanaticism of the Young Pioneers [the official East German youth group]."

Before leaving Checkpoint Charlie and crossing into the former Soviet sector, stop in at **Cafe Adler**, at which John le Carré and other spymasters found some of the best seats to watch the Cold War. We recommend that you save Museum Haus am Checkpoint Charlie, which also has excellent pieces of wall art, for a later time.

From Checkpoint Charlie, proceed through the former border area along Friedrichstrasse toward Leipziger Strasse. Once released by the East German border police, visitors found themselves on this deserted stretch of Friedrichstrasse. Wooden fences, dingy concrete structures, and crumbling brick buildings, which had long ago lost their fanciful sandstone façades, gave this area the look of a haphazard construction project that was never quite finished. Today, cranes and scaffolding promise a quicker pace of transformation but continue to give the street an improvised, indefinite character.

Friedrichstrasse is one of the most famous streets in Berlin in part because it always has been true to the transitory nature of the city. Since being laid out by the Prussian kings at the end of the seventeenth century, it has witnessed all the city's dramatic renovations. Originally a courtly residential avenue lined with homes and shops, in the middle of the nineteenth century it became a busy commercial thoroughfare with hotels and offices. By 1900, Friedrichstrasse boasted 250 cafes and restaurants and had become renowned for its adventurous nightlife, which Expressionist painters Ludwig Meidner and Ernst Ludwig Kirchner depicted in their sharp-edged portraits. It was a place of "large feather hats, of feather boas and high-laced bodices," remembered the bitter, brilliant Weimar-era artist George Grosz.

After Germany's defeat in World War I, Friedrich-strasse slipped into a period of long-lasting decline. Elegant Berlin had moved over to the Kurfürstendamm, never to return here. In his novel, *Wolf unter Wölfen*, Hans Fallada described the tawdry street that remained in the 1920s: "It was almost one after the other on the sidewalk: hustlers, beggars, prostitutes . . . Against the sides of houses, beggars sat, crouched, or lay—they were all war cripples if you believed the signs they carried . . . Blind men blubbered in pitiless monotones. Shudderers shook their arms or their heads. War wounds were on public display." World War II and the postwar division of the city sealed the fate of Friedrichstrasse. The chic shops and Western bank branches that have recently opened alongside the Grand Hotel anticipate a prosperous future for this midtown avenue, but the future has not quite arrived.

Walk past the brand-new buildings to Taubenstrasse, turn right, and head toward the splendid eighteenth-century **Gendarmenmarkt**. (Construction might force you to turn right one block earlier, at Mohrenstrasse). To proud Berliners, the Gendarmenmarkt is the most beautiful square in Europe. The hyperbole of local patriots aside, it is a remarkable urban arena, with two cathedrals flanking the restored **Schauspielhaus**, or Royal Playhouse. Named after the *Gens d'armes* regiment, which had its stables and guardhouse here from 1736 to 1782, the elongated square was originally conceived as the chief marketplace of *Friedrichstadt*, a new neighborhood built by the Great Elector Friedrich Wilhelm. (Prussia's rulers were only designated kings by the Holy Roman Emperor in 1701, at which point the Roman enumeration of electors ended and a new series of kings began.)

After the ruinous end of the Thirty Years' War in 1648, which left Berlin with fewer than six thousand inhabitants and emptied state coffers, Friedrich Wilhelm (who reigned from 1640–1688) embarked on a program of thorough militarization in an effort to make Prussia immune from further foreign invasions. In 1657 the Great Elector stationed a permanent garrison in the city, and to pay for the standing army, he revamped the city into a reliable source of revenue. The crown imposed heavy duties on all goods that entered the city at the Brandenburg, Potsdam, and other tollgates. In addition, the Great Elector encouraged foreign entrepreneurs—first Calvinists from Holland, then Huguenots from France, and also a group of wealthy Viennese Jews—to settle the outskirts of Berlin.

To accommodate these newcomers and the garrison, new neighborhoods were laid out. The largest of these was Friedrichstadt. Look at a map and you can still see the strict geometry of the area (the hand of royal absolutism), a contrast to the crooked paths that lead through Berlin's medieval core around the Spree River. During a visit to Berlin in 1804, Madame de Staël, the famous French essayist, noted that the streets were "very broad and perfectly straight," the houses handsome, and the general appearance "regular." "Berlin is an entirely modern city," she continued, "nothing of the antique interrupts the uniformity." Berlin seems "destined only for the convenient assemblage of pleasure and industry."

Madame de Staël neglected to mention the pronounced military aspect of Friedrichstadt, however. Long and broad avenues swept up from parade grounds: Unter den Linden from the *Quarre* (now Pariser Platz), Leipziger Strasse from the *Achteck* (Leipziger Platz, adjacent to Potsdamer Platz), and Friedrichstrasse from the *Rondell* (Mehringplatz). The blocks of Friedrichstadt were so uniform that one Berliner, Daniel Amadeus Atterbom, thought he was strolling among military barracks. Indeed, he noted in 1817, "almost at any conceivable spot, boys in uniform are stood at attention with an officer shouting 'One!—Two!—Halt!—Right Face!—About Face!' " Looking at these regular streets a few years later, Ernst Dronke, a nineteenth-century social critic, knew right away that "a revolution was not possible." "Physiognomy is the mirror of the soul," he wrote, and Berliners were loyal monarchists. A failed revolution did break out a few years later, in 1848, and again in 1918, but the spirit if not the letter of Dronke's observation held true.

For over three hundred years, immigrants have figured prominently in Berlin's history. Most important to the city were Jewish newcomers' (whose contributions are recounted in Walk 2), Turkish migrants (who are discussed in Walk 4), and the French Huguenots, who built their homes in this area, around Friedrichstrasse. After 1685, when Louis XIV revoked the Edict of Nantes that had protected French Protestants from persecution, French refugees poured into Central Europe. For the most part skilled artisans, the Huguenots were a boon to backward Prussian manufactures. To attract these prosperous immigrants, Friedrich Wilhelm promised them land, economic concessions, and a high degree of cultural and municipal autonomy. Eventually six thousand Huguenots settled among the fifteen thousand residents of Berlin. By 1700 almost every third Berliner spoke French, and many more ate the asparagus, cauliflower, and artichokes the French had introduced. "They tempered our raw customs," recalled Carl Ludwig von Pöllnitz, master of ceremonies at the court. It should be remembered that foreigners—first from France, later from Poland, and today from Turkey—have always enriched this city.

With its own town hall, hospitals, courts, churches, and schools, the Huguenot community prospered until 1809 when liberal ideas of a free and equal citizenry dissolved special privileges and emancipated previously sanctioned groups such as the Jews. The influence of the French is still evident, however. Berlin boasts a French gymnasium, an elite high school, and the city's vocabulary is peppered with French words.

On the Gendarmenmarkt, the twin towers of the Lutheran **Deutscher Dom** (on the left as you look at the theater) and the Calvinist **Französischer Dom** (on the right), each exactly 230 feet high, underscored the religious tolerance and cultural pluralism of eighteenth-century Berlin. "*Hier mus ein jeder nach seiner Fassung Selich werden*" (All should find bliss after their own fashion), wrote Frederick the Great (who reigned from 1740–1786). The churches themselves date from 1701–8, but Frederick had the towers added in 1780–85 in an attempt to give Berlin a more worldly aspect. Frederick the Great enhanced the square further by clearing out the stables of the *Gens d'armes* regiment and adding a theater between the two churches.

The towers are vanity pieces and serve no religious function; indeed, visitors can climb the 254 steps to the top of the Französischer Dom to survey the city. Helpful signs along the balustrade identify the sights (open Tuesday through Saturday, 10 am to 4 pm). At the top of the dome you can literally have ringside seats and watch the *Glockenspieler* at work during daily concerts (the bells chime automatically at 12, 3, and 7, and are actually played on Tuesdays at 2 pm and Saturday at 3 pm). You'll want to repay your efforts with beer or wine and a snack at the lovely wood-paneled **Turmstuben** (only 81 steps up and open daily, 12 pm to 1 am). Historical photos of the city line the walls to the top of the dome, and on the ground floor there is a small but first-class Huguenot Museum containing documents, religious texts, and prints (open Monday through Saturday, 12 pm to 5 pm; Sunday, 1 pm to 5 pm).

A grand Schauspielhaus was erected in 1817 by Carl Gotthard Langhans (who also designed the Brandenburger Tor). It was here that the patriotic opera by Karl Maria

Schauspielhaus

von Weber about the *Freischütz*, the volunteers who fought Napoleon, premiered in 1821. A year later, however, Langhans's theater burned down; it was rebuilt in neoclassical style by Berlin's leading architect Karl Friedrich Schinkel. To honor the role of the arts in the very military capital, Schinkel insisted on an imposing Ionian portico and a flight of steps, but these do not even lead to the entrance, which is well hidden beneath the stairs. Unfortunately, the result cramps both the building and the square. The marble statue of Friedrich Schiller, who ranks with Goethe as Germany's greatest writer, was placed in front of the theater in 1871. Later, the Nazis carted off Schiller because he stood for humanist traditions they had repudiated, but he was safely returned when the war-damaged Schauspielhaus reopened as a concert hall in 1988.

It is easy to recount the architectural follies of the former German Democratic Republic. The destruction of the Hohenzollern palace and important buildings by Schinkel seems incomprehensible today. But when the state decided to restore prewar monuments, as in the case of the Gendarmenmarkt, it did so expertly. Before leaving the Schauspielhaus, walk over to the left side of the stairs; just in front of the flagpoles and embedded in the tiled square are plaques remembering Berlin audiences, with quotes from Schiller, Beethoven, and Otto Nagel, a well-known proletarian artist. The rightmost plaque is missing, however, an indication that history is constantly being rewritten in Berlin. Until 1989 it read:

> *Buchstablich aus Ruinen auferstanden, wird das Berlin von heute immer mehr zum Symbol für den Siegeszug des Sozialismus auf dem deutschen Boden.*

> Arisen literally out of ruins, Berlin today is becoming ever more a symbol for the triumph of socialism on German soil.
>
> Erich Honecker

With its Saturday morning market, theater, and twin towers, the Gendarmenmarkt attested to the civic virtues of Berlin. By the beginning of the nineteenth century, the city boasted over 100,000 inhabitants and attracted writers and philosophers from across German-speaking Europe. Rahel Varnhagen's famous literary salon of German Romantics met in Friedrichstadt, at Französische Strasse 20. E.T.A. Hoffmann, whose stories have been adapted into Offenbach's opera *Tales of Hoffmann* and Tchaikovsky's ballet *The Nutcracker Suite*, lived across from this marketplace, at the corner of Tauben and Charlottenstrasse, on the north side of the Friedrichstadt-Passage. In the 1820s and 1830s, Hoffmann, Heinrich Heine, and other intellectuals met in the convivial wine restaurant Lutter & Wegner that once stood beyond the Französischer Dom, on the corner of Französischer and Charlottenstrasse. Nearby, on Jägerstrasse, the Lesekonditorei Stehely nourished young revolutionaries Karl Marx, Friedrich Engels, and Ludwig Feuerbach with a rich assortment of newspapers as well as pastries. Sadly, industrial development, World War II, and the division of Berlin snuffed out the bustling urban scenery of the Gendarmenmarkt, although cafes, restaurants, and bookstores are reviving the square today. If you'd like to take a break before moving on, two comfortable cafes can be found on Charlottenstrasse behind the Schauspielhaus: *Cafe Möhring* and *Arkade*. Around the corner, at Französischer Strasse 47, you will find the elegant brasserie *Borchardt*. And on the corner of Jägerstrasse and Markengraftstrasse there is a fine upscale restaurant, *Französischer Hof.*

The life of cities ebbs and flows, as Hoffmann perceived while observing the busy market activity from his window on Taubenstrasse. The Gendarmenmarkt provided "a true picture of life's constant change," he wrote in his story "Cousin's Corner Window." "Great activity and pressing needs bring masses of people together, but after a few moments, everything is desolate. The voices that had mixed into an incoherent din have fallen still, and each abandoned spot exclaims a horrible 'it once was' all too clearly."

Exit the Gendarmenmarkt by going right on Französischer Strasse (behind the Französischer Dom) and walk toward Marx-Engels-Platz. The dusty and desolate street echoes Hoffmann's refrain: "It once was." You see around you not only the pockmarked façades of prewar Berlin but also the last monuments of an older, preindustrial city and, not far off, the already decaying glass-and-concrete palaces of East German state socialism. As Französischer Strasse passes into Werderstrasse you will see on your left the **Friedrichswerder Kirche**, which was designed by Schinkel in 1824 to fit the district's medieval character. Now only this church remains as a remembrance of the old neighborhood.

The narrow, cluttered streets around the city core did not leave room for an imposing cathedral, so Schinkel opted for the simpler lines of an English chapel. Although the Friedrichswerder Church seems, at first glance, completely different from Schinkel's Schauspielhaus four blocks away, both designs rely on classical shapes and cubist proportions. While the clean lines of the church honor the classical tradition with which Prussia's educated middle classes identified, the unadorned red-brick walls also suggest Germany's medieval heritage. Brick has a patriotic aspect as well. It is the building block of almost all Berlin; there are no natural stone deposits in the marshy plains that surround the city. Behind the impressively sculptured sandstone façades on buildings throughout Berlin is plain old brick, which Schinkel grew fond of. He argued that exposed brick and unpretentious terra-cotta adornments would give Berlin a distinctive architectural style. Striking a universal as well as a local patriotic note, the spare brickwork of the Friedrichswerder Church became Schinkel's signature. The **Schinkel Museum** is located inside the vaulted and roomy space of the former church (open Wednesday through Sunday, 9 am to 5 pm).

Across Werderstrasse is a monument to the promiscuity of twentieth-century bureaucracy. Built in 1934–38 as the first large architectural project commissioned by the Nazis, this giant complex housed the powerful **Reichsbank** (state bank), the East German Finance Ministry, and, after 1959, the Central Committee of the Socialist Unity Party, the official name of the East German Communists. Heinrich Wolff designed the Reichsbank building in typically monumental style, although Walter Gropius and Ludwig Mies van der Rohe—Bauhaus architects whom we usually associate with opponents of Nazism—initially sought an accommodation with the regime and put forward designs of their own. The building is now empty, waiting for the federal Ministry of the Interior to move from Bonn to Berlin; the Communists, who still carry on as the Party of Democratic Socialism, have moved into the more modest Karl-Liebknecht-Haus on Rosa-Luxemburg-Platz, a building that had served as Communist Party headquarters before 1933 (see Walk 3).

Before crossing the Spree Kanal on Werderstrasse, you will see on your left another of the giant boxes of East German officialdom: East Germany's Ministry of Foreign Affairs, which closed its doors on October 3, 1990, the day of German reunification. The ministry is a reminder that no self-respecting state can be without its assemblage of ugly modern buildings. After much protest, it was built in 1965 on the site of Schinkel's masterly **Bauakademie** (Academy of Architecture), a building finished with exposed brick and embellished with terra-cotta rather than sandstone ornaments. (Some remnants survive as adornments to the Schinkelklause, behind the Operncafe, farther along on this walk.) The now empty ministry is scheduled to be torn down.

As you cross the Spree on the **Schleusenbrücke**, note the metal relief plates that depict the early years of Berlin settlement. The ones with the dates 1650 and 1688 were created by artist Kurt Schumacher who was executed by the Nazis for his resistance activities in 1942. The Nazis overlooked these plates when they went about destroying his art. Looking to your right, you can also see the iron **Jungfernbrücke** (1798), the oldest surviving drawbridge in Berlin.

The architectural showpiece of East German modernism is the **Palast der Republik**, the orange box ahead of you across Marx-Engels-Platz. With cafes and restaurants, theaters, discotheques, a bowling alley, and a closet large enough for five thousand coats (as a pre-1989 guide boasts), "palaces" like this, which was colloquially known as *Palazzo Prozzo*, added "class" to socialist culture and can be found throughout former East Germany. The palace also housed the compliant East German parliament. For all the extravagance and pomp (the palace took one thousand days to complete and decorate), the interior was insulated with asbestos, and as a result the building is closed and has an uncertain future.

At the time of reunification there were dreamers who

Schleusenbrücke

wanted to undo Communism by dismantling all signs of its former existence. Wouldn't it be cheaper, they asked, to simply tear down rather than clean up the Palace of the Republic? And in its place they rather seriously offered proposals to rebuild the Hohenzollern Palace that had stood here until 1951. The palace stood between the two arms of the Spree and occupied this entire square. The two interior courtyards of the palace are now a parking lot and sometime carnival ground.

History cannot be undone, of course, and the old palace will probably never be rebuilt; indeed, it looks as if Germany's new foreign ministry will be erected here instead. Nonetheless, the memory of the Hohenzollern *Schloss* intrigues Berliners, who were always fascinated by the goings-on *bei Kaisers*. Although heavily damaged in one of the last bombing raids of the war, its massive stone walls remained standing, and the palace could have been renovated. The imposing fortress was also a superlative example of baroque architecture, featuring the work

62

of Andreas Schlüter (the architect who completed the Zeughaus that we will see a bit later on Unter den Linden) and Johann Friedrich Eosander. Moreover, the royal palace was an inseparable part of Berlin. Portions of the imperial residence had stood along the banks of the Spree River since 1443. It, along with the medieval city hall— exactly where the *Rotes Rathaus* sits today—and the old stone churches, Saint Nicolai and Saint Marien (both of which have been restored), were the core of the old city (see Walk 3).

The palace may have housed the stern and often inept Hohenzollern kings, but it also played a large role in Berlin's struggles for freedom. After all, the people had surrounded the royal palace on March 19, 1848, presented King Friedrich Wilhelm IV with the bodies of citizens who had fallen the night before in street battles with royal troops, and forced the monarch to endorse constitutional reform. In November 1918, just prior to Germany's defeat in World War I, revolutionaries chased the kaiser out of the palace and the country altogether. Socialist workers and revolutionary troops occupied this and other imperial buildings, and the fiery Spartakus leader Karl Liebknecht proclaimed the Socialist Republic from a palace balcony in the late afternoon of November 9, 1918. Although postwar Germany became a democratic rather than a Soviet-style socialist republic—it developed along the lines envisaged by moderate socialists who had proclaimed a parliamentary republic two hours earlier from the Reichstag, which sits at the other end of Unter den Linden—Liebknecht's proclamation eventually had immense political significance. For East Germans, his balcony speech represented the historical legitimacy of the division of the country by distinguishing real Communism from the watered-down democratic socialism that had supposedly watched helplessly as Hitler rose to power and then compromised itself needlessly with capitalist reconstruction after World War II.

When the palace ruins were finally cleared away in

1951, to underscore the Communists' new beginning, the balcony and surrounding portal from where Liebknecht had spoken were preserved and embedded into the façade of the **Staatsrat** (State Council) building on the south side of Marx-Engels-Platz (to your right as you face the Palace of the Republic). Historians sometimes claim that the balcony is directly opposite its original location, overlooking what had been the narrow Schlossplatz. The balcony that had been preserved, however, is Portal IV, which was designed by Eosander in 1713. Before it was stamped into the Staatsrat building, the portal overlooked the Lustgarten, a far larger square north of the palace; it is where the large socialist crowds gathered that gray November afternoon three-quarters of a century ago.

Walk over Marx-Engels-Platz toward the **Lustgarten**, keeping the Spree Kanal to your left. To get to the Lustgarten, carefully cross the busy six-lane avenue at Schlossbrücke (we will discuss the bridge a bit later). The tiled square in front of the museum and cathedral is a remnant of the Lustgarten, which was laid out in 1573 as orchards and kitchen gardens to provision the palace. In 1653 Great Elector Friedrich Wilhelm had the Lustgarten redesigned as a park after the Dutch fashion. However, the pleasant paths and exotic plants were leveled in 1730 by Prussia's "Soldier King," Friedrich Wilhelm I. The Lustgarten became a parade ground for Prussian troops, and for a time civilians were prohibited from even crossing the square. A more relaxed code followed in 1832 when Peter Josef Lenné (a city planner) restored the garden's parklike character, although military concerts were held every afternoon, weather permitting, after the changing of the guard on Unter den Linden.

It was in the Lustgarten that crowds gathered in June 1871 to view French weaponry captured during the Franco-Prussian War; to celebrate the kaiser and the coming of war in August 1914; and also to hear Liebknecht proclaim a socialist republic little more than four years later. In June 1922 hundreds of thousands of Berliners poured into the Lustgarten to demonstrate against anti-Semitism after the assassination of Foreign Minister Walther Rathenau. The Nazis put an end to the demonstrations of the Weimar democracy, however, and in 1935 Hitler ordered the garden's trees cut down, the immense seventy-five-ton granite basin removed, and the square tiled as a spacious parade ground for his remilitarized Germany. Although the basin is back, the stony Lustgarten looks pretty much as it did in the 1930s. And in November 1992 hundreds of thousands of Berliners returned to the Lustgarten to demonstrate against anti-Semitism and racism after months of neo-Nazi activity.

Whether as park or parade ground, the Lustgarten has been a mirror of changing political intentions and cultural values. The most ambitious attempt to give a permanent role to the square was undertaken by Karl Friedrich Schinkel when he built the **Altes Museum**, directly ahead of you on the north side of the Lustgarten. We have encountered Schinkel throughout this walk, and with good reason: He ranks as Berlin's most important architect, having rebuilt the city between 1820 and 1840, much as Baron von Haussmann rebuilt Paris a generation later. Schinkel's ambition was to fashion Berlin into a cultural as well as a military capital; he wanted to yoke Athens to Sparta.

The beginning of the nineteenth century, after Prussia had endured its most serious political crisis, offered Schinkel a splendid opportunity. Defeated by Napoleon at Jena in 1806, the Prussian state almost disappeared from the European map. However, the final defeat of the French at Waterloo in 1815 revived Prussia's international position, but only comprehensive internal reform restored political stability at home. More rational state administration, equality under the law, and new universities promised Prussians a brighter future. At the same time, the victory over the French infused Prussians with a sense of being German. Schinkel was anxious to further the cause of reform and to nourish national feeling. The Altes Museum served both ends.

The huge procession that made its way up Unter den Linden to celebrate the defeat of Napoleon in 1814 displayed the treasures that the French had plundered in 1806. Thousands of Berliners came out to cheer the victorious troops and also to marvel at the art that previously had been locked away in the castles and palaces of the nobility. The proposal to build a museum, the first of its kind in Prussia, sought to sustain popular nationalism by permanently exhibiting German art. By moving art from private, exclusively aristocratic circles into the public realm, a museum would express the rising self-confidence of the middle classes and involve the people in the fate of the nation. And by placing the Altes Museum on the Lustgarten, across from the palace and between the Berliner Dom (cathedral) and the Zeughaus (the arsenal across the river), Schinkel highlighted the importance of national culture and national identity. In this constellation, art joined the monarchy, the church, and the military as one of the four pillars of the Prussian state.

Schinkel was no revolutionary. He built summer homes for Prussian nobles, redesigned rooms in the palace, and revamped the old cathedral. A commoner by birth, Schinkel (1781–1841) regarded the achievements of the middle classes as equal to the refinements of the aristocracy. He therefore made sure that the Altes Museum would be architecturally able to hold its ground in face of the overawing palace across the way. He designed a monumental classical façade and a portico of eighteen Ionic columns to express the power and strength of this bougeois institution. The flight of high steps literally lifts the visitor to the realm of the arts. An interior rotunda allowed for meditation and sanctuary. The slow, measured movement from outside to inside added to the pretensions of the museum. Unfortunately the glass front that has since been added to keep out drafts disrupts this effect.

Over the course of the nineteenth century, the Altes Museum (opened in 1831) became part of a museum complex, the *Museumsinsel*, which included the Neues Museum (1855), the National Gallery (1876), the Bode Museum (1904), and the magnificent Pergamon Museum (1930). For all its virtues, the Museumsinsel shifted the center of gravity away from Unter den Linden and the Lustgarten, an unintentional thwarting of Schinkel's desire to put art at the center of the political stage. The museum complex received several direct bomb hits during the air raids of February 3, 1945. To this day the Neues Museum remains under reconstruction. The Altes Museum was slowly but expertly restored by the East Germans and today houses temporary exhibitions. The museums here are all worth visiting—especially the Pergamon, which is located behind the Altes Museum. We suggest, however, that you reserve a day for them alone so you don't rush your experience of their collections.

As the placement of the Altes Museum reveals, Schinkel did more than design buildings—he fashioned urban arenas. Schinkel hoped to create for Berlin a civic culture in which citizens would prosper. His Berlin was always more than simply a parade ground. But the idea of an emancipated and self-confident metropolis did not always sit well with the Hohenzollerns. The last kaiser, Wilhelm II (who reigned from 1888–1918), despised Schinkel's measured work and redesigned Berlin as a grand imperial showpiece. Turn-of-the-century architects used pompously sculpted sandstone façades to cover the local red brick that Schinkel and his students had favored, and they erected colossal monuments where Schinkel had preferred classically proportioned ones.

There is no better example of Wilhelm's grandiose architectural tastes than the newly restored **Berliner Dom** on the east side of the Lustgarten (to the right of the Altes Museum). This cathedral is a typically Wilhelmine construction; it is too large, too ornate, too restless. Berliners jokingly referred to it as the *Seelengasometer*—gasometer for souls. Built in 1894–1905 by Julius Raschdorff, the

Schlossbrücke, Berliner Dom, and Fernsehtum

cathedral is dominated by a huge central dome, 374 feet high, that is enhanced by four corner cupolas, whereas its predecessor, a modest church commissioned by Frederick the Great, had only one cupola and two towers, not nearly enough for the great world power into which Wilhelm II wanted to transform Germany. "We are destined for greatness, and I will lead you to wonderful days yet," he proclaimed in 1892. This was someone who, according to Bismarck, the former chancellor, "wanted to have a birthday party every day of his life." The newly restored Berliner Dom is open Monday through Saturday, 9 am to 5 pm, and Sunday, 12 pm to 5 pm; tours are held on Wednesday at 3 pm.

From the Berliner Dom, walk back across the Lustgarten. The concrete **memorial cube** that you see ahead on the street side of the square was erected by the East Germans. It declares eternal friendship with the Soviet Union and commemorates German Communists who on May 18, 1942, torched the Nazis' anti-Soviet exhibit, *The Soviet Paradise*, which had been erected here to inflame public opinion in the second year of the long war against

Russia. Led by thirty-year-old Herbert Baum, who had endured a difficult underground life as both a Jew and a Communist, the anti-Nazi activists were rounded up four days later and executed.

At the end of the Lustgarten, cross the **Schloss-brücke**, or palace bridge, to **Unter den Linden**, which means "Under the Lindens," the famous tree-lined boulevard of old Berlin. For a long time Prussian kings crossed the Spree here on a narrow wooden bridge. Old city maps refer to it as Dogs Bridge since this is where the royal hounds were assembled before hunting parties headed into the Tiergarten. King Friedrich Wilhelm III finally commissioned Schinkel to design a bridge commensurate with the beauty and breadth of Unter den Linden. Schinkel conceived of the Schlossbrücke (completed in 1824) not simply as a byway for traffic but as an entrance onto the *Schlossinsel*, the Spree River island that was the site of the Hohenzollern palace and of royal power. Four large pedestals and statues on either side of the bridge create an impressive interior space and commemorate the patriotic struggles of Germany against France. On the left side, the Goddess of Victory teaches the boy warrior the history of the heroes, Athena instructs him in the use of weapons and presents him with arms, and Victory crowns the conquerer. On the right side, Victory holds the wounded warrior, Athena protects him and urges him to rejoin the battle, and finally Iris leads the fallen warrior to Olympus. When the East Germans returned these martial statues to their pedestals in the 1980s, and a mounted Frederick the Great to Unter den Linden, just down the boulevard, it was clear that the socialist new beginning was casting about aimlessly for historical legitimacy.

Prussian militarism dominates the top of Unter den Linden, the grand east-west axis that sweeps down to the Brandenburger Tor, past the Tiergarten, into western Brandenburg. Walk on the right-hand side, past the **Zeughaus**, or arsenal (1695–1706), one of the few remaining baroque structures in Berlin (the city museum on Lindenstrasse in Kreuzberg is another).

Until 1875 the Zeughaus warehoused cannons and muskets; thereafter, it displayed them as a museum. After World War II the Zeughaus became a very didactic Museum of German History in which modern times naturally culminated in the formation of the German Democratic Republic. Dismantled in 1990, a year that swept aside so much official socialist culture, the museum is undergoing a significant overhaul and will reopen in 1995 as the major history museum of newly reunified Germany. What is really worth seeing, then as now, are "Schlüter's masks," the twenty-two heads of dying warriors designed by Andreas Schlüter at the end of the seventeenth century. They are to be found over the portals in the museum's interior courtyard and depict a compassion and tenderness in time of war that does not square with our usual ideas about Prussia. But Schlüter, a Danziger by birth and a Mennonite by conviction, was not a typical Prussian anyhow. Helmets and suits of armor, which correspond to the masks, adorn the building's exterior façade.

Continue down the right-hand side of Unter den Linden, past the Zeughaus, to the **Neue Wache**. Back when East was East and West was West, the Neue Wache, or new guardhouse, featured the changing of the guard with goose-stepping soldiers of the socialist People's Army. The paradox of this very Prussian parade step (with all its discomforting Nazi-era reminders), in front of a memorial commemorating the victims of militarism, drew hundreds of visitors. We think we saw one of the guards smile once, when he was affectionately teased by a pretty passerby, but that was in 1990. Otherwise, the Neue Wache has always put on a very somber face. Constructed in 1816–18, the first work by Schinkel, the guardhouse commemorated the Wars of Liberation against Napoleon. Strained Prussian finances kept Schinkel from completing the building as designed; the sides and the back reveal red brick that is so untidily laid, it obviously was not meant to be exposed. Schinkel liked the effect, however, and incorporated it into future projects.

In 1931, President Hindenburg rededicated the Neue Wache to the memory of German soldiers killed in World War I. Damage from the next world war was repaired in 1957 when the site reopened with an eternal flame as a memorial to the victims of fascism and militarism. The guardhouse now contains a recast Käthe Kollwitz sculpture, *Pietà*, and serves as a national monument dedicated "To the Victims of War and Tyranny." In whatever form, the building serves as a reminder not to take the choreographed patriotism of any regime too seriously. This lesson was never taught better than on October 16, 1906, when Wilhelm Voigt, an unemployed drifter, bought a Prussian captain's uniform from a secondhand dealer, commandeered a troop of passing soldiers, and ordered them to Köpenick, a Berlin suburb. At the city hall, Voigt arrested the startled but compliant mayor and signed a receipt for the 4,002 marks and 37 pfennigs in the municipal cash box. Voigt then returned to Berlin, delivered the hapless mayor to the Neue Wache around seven in the evening, and disappeared into the night, forever amusing the world with the reminder of how much Germans respected the sight of a uniform.

At this point you might want to take a break to reflect on this *Köpenickiade* and other peculiarities of German history. A good stopping point is the outdoor cafe and restaurant across the street, **Operncafe**. As you carefully cross busy Unter den Linden, swing by the **statue of Frederick the Great** on horseback. It stands right in the middle of the boulevard. Here, at five in the afternoon on July 31, 1914, a lieutenant and four drummers stood at attention. After a drumroll, the lieutenant read the order announcing the mobilization of the German army. That same afternoon, Kaiser Wilhelm II spoke from the palace. "We are being forced to defend ourselves," he told thousands of anxious Germans, "the sword is being pressed into our hands. I urge you to go to church, to kneel before God, and to plead with Him to aid our courageous army." The next day, Germany declared war on Russia. World War I had begun.

The pedestal is ringed with famous contemporaries of "old Fritz," including the eminent philosophers Gotthold Ephraim Lessing and Immanuel Kant, who pose beneath the horse's hindquarters—such was the status of philosophy in this garrison state. Indeed, Frederick the Great once called the university "His Majesty's intellectual regiment of the guards." Even so, Prussians cherished Frederick the Great. When this statue by Christian Rauch was finally unveiled in May 1851, an anonymous pamphleteer appealed to the long-dead king:

> *Alter Fritz, steig Du hernieder*
> *und regier die Preussen wieder.*
> *Lass in diesen schlechten Zeiten,*
> *Lieber Friedrich Wilhelm reiten.*

> Old Fritz, come on down
> and rule the Prussians once again.
> In these terrible times,
> please let Friedrich Wilhelm ride.

Frederick the Great remained mounted, however, and so joined scores of kings, poets, and generals immortalized in stone around Berlin. The 1912 Baedeker, for example, indexed more than 80 monuments worth seeing. In the Tiergarten, on the other side of the Brandenburger Tor, a *Siegesallee* (Victory Alley) of 32 famous and not so famous Hohenzollerns constituted another of Wilhelm II's contributions to the imperial capital. "Who shows the greatest appreciation of art?" Berliners asked after the so-called *Puppenallee*, or Alley of Dolls, was dedicated in 1901. "Whoever runs past it the fastest" was the response. According to another satirist, the imperial capital boasted 232 monuments, depicting a total of 716 people and 128 animals, "as of July 1, 1905, at 6 am." Didn't one city tour even mark the spot in the Tiergarten where there was no monument yet?

More statues await you in the small park beside the Operncafe: Scharnhorst, Yorck, Gneisenau, and Blücher—all generals from the Wars of Liberation. But let's go to the Operncafe first. At the stands outside you can order grilled sausages and *Berliner Weisse*—beer with a dash of refreshing red raspberry or green woodruff syrup (*rot* or *grün*)—and settle yourself at one of the outdoor tables. Or go inside to the fancier restaurant to sample the glorious desserts and small meals. The restaurant is in what was once known as the *Prinzessinnenpalais*, a baroque palace built in 1733 that got its name in 1811 when the three daughters of King Friedrich Wilhelm III moved in.

From the Operncafe, stay on the left-hand side of Unter den Linden and proceed past the opera house to **Opern-platz**, the broad plaza on the west side of the opera. Opernplatz was the realization of Frederick the Great's dream to recreate the spatial glory of ancient Rome in Prussian Berlin. Designed by his favorite architect, Georg Wenzeslaus von Knobelsdorff, this square, once known as the *Forum Fridericianum*, is flanked on the left by the **Staatsoper**, the first public opera in Prussia (1743), and on the right by the Old Royal Library (built in 1775–80), a rococo structure that has always been called the **Kommode**, or chest of drawers. In 1807 the philosopher Johann Gottlieb Fichte delivered his flaming patriotic appeal against the French occupiers, *Reden an die deutsche Nation* (Addresses to the German Nation), in the library's auditorium. He appealed to his audience "to have character and be German." This proud but rather chauvinistic statement marked the birth of German nationalism. In the back left corner of the plaza is **Hedwigskirche**, a domed Roman Catholic cathedral modeled on the Roman Pantheon, for which the Protestant king laid the cornerstone in 1747. (Saint Hedwig is the patron saint of Silesia, a territory conquered by Prussia in the eighteenth century.)

Across Unter den Linden you can see the main building of **Humboldt University**, which Frederick the Great built in 1766 as the new Hohenzollern palace. It was originally intended to complete the *Forum Fridericianum*. Unfortunately, the building is completely separated from Opernplatz by high railings and by the busy boulevard, so the effect of an ancient forum is lost. As it happened, Frederick the Great lost interest in Berlin and refused to move into the newly built residence; instead, he concentrated his architectural energies on his beloved *Sanssouci* in Potsdam. He eventually passed the palace on to his brother, Prince Heinrich. In 1810, as part of the reforms that followed the state's defeat by Napoleon's armies, the princely residence became the site of Friedrich-Wilhelm University (since 1946 it has been known as Humboldt University after its intellectual founder Wilhelm von Humboldt). It was here that Hegel occupied the chair in philosophy from 1817 to 1831. The most famous student was surely Karl Marx, who attended the university from 1836 to 1841 and whose spirit still lingers. If you enter the main building, you'll be greeted by Marx's famous injunction: "Philosophers have hitherto explained the world; it is now time to alter it."

In World War II the opera, the library, and Saint Hedwig's were all gutted by fire, but the first embers of the conflagration were lit much earlier—on a rainy Wednesday, May 10, 1933, when Nazi students from the university burned piles of modernist classics on the Opernplatz. Books by Thomas Mann, Alfred Döblin, Sigmund Freud, and many others were pulled from library shelves and thrown into the flames. Although the great nineteenth-century German-Jewish poet Heinrich Heine (1797–1856) had prophesied that once books were burned, people would soon follow, the world took the notorious actions on the Opernplatz rather in stride.

Indeed, Germany had never been so popular for tourists than during the Nazi period. Berlin, which hosted the summer Olympic Games in 1936, enjoyed record numbers of overnight stays in the mid-1930s. The city was accordingly transformed into a showcase for Nazism. All the old trees on Unter den Linden, for example, were cut down to make way for a more spacious and imposing parade route. Tourists who stayed in fine hotels along the broad avenue—in the Bristol, the Adlon, or the Carleton—did not see what they did not wish to see. But a few Berliners remembered the old revue hit sung by Claire Waldoff: *So lang noch Unter den Linden / Die alten Bäume blühn / Kann nichts uns überwinden / Berlin bleibt doch Berlin.* (As long as the old trees blossom on Unter den Linden, nothing can beat us; Berlin will remain Berlin.) Berlin under the swastika was not the same, however. After 1938, German Jews were no longer permitted to stroll the Linden from the university to the Zeughaus or walk down Wilhelmstrasse or go to movies or amusement parks.

From Opernplatz, continue down Unter den Linden to the corner of Friedrichstrasse. Before 1933, Unter den Linden was Berlin's grand avenue, with the best hotels and restaurants, and at this intersection, the lively **Kranzler Eck**, elegant cafes—where one was never too early or too late—brimmed with conversations, arguments, and flirtations. Coffeehouses first established themselves in the 1830s and welcomed strollers and idlers; they permitted smoking, which was not allowed on the very proper Unter den Linden until after the 1848 Revolution. With Cafe Bauer (which once stood on the southeast corner) and Cafe Kranzler (on the southwest), this corner of Friedrichstrasse and Unter den Linden quickly became among the busiest in Berlin. Here, the demimonde crossed the path of high society. Just a few hundred paces to the left or right of this once-vibrant intersection was enough to assault the senses. Walter Kiaulehn, in his history, *Berlin: Destiny of a World City*, described this cosmopolitan place: ". . . cacophonous rings of traffic signals, melodies from organ grinders, cries of newspaper vendors, and the bell of Bolle's milkmen, voices of fruit and vegetable sellers, hoarse utterings of beggars, whispers of easy women, the low roar of streetcars and their screech against the old iron tracks, and millions of steps dragging, trippling, pounding. At the same time, a kaleidoscope of colorful sights . . . neon lights, the bright electric lights of offices and factories . . . lanterns on horse-drawn carts and automobiles, arc-lighting, light bulbs, carbide lamps." Unter den Linden certainly does not compare today. The only building on the corner to survive the war is the **Switzerland House** on the northwest corner, which was built in 1936.

Farther down Unter den Linden is the long stretch of the **Russian embassy**, built partially with marble retrieved from Hitler's New Chancellory that the Soviets blew up in 1945. This imposing complex attests to the crucial role played by the once powerful patron of East Germany, but it also compounds the prevailing lifelessness of the avenue. Before passing on, look at the handsome bust of Lenin in the courtyard. Outside the embassy, street peddlers sell souvenirs and military paraphernalia of the former Soviet empire.

Another block farther and you arrive in front of perhaps the most famous gate in the world, **Brandenburger Tor**, the triumphal entryway into Berlin. There is no more evocative symbol of German power than this simple six-columned neoclassical gate built by Carl Gotthard Langhans in 1791. Foreign conquerers from Napoleon in 1806 to the Soviets in 1945, and victorious German troops throughout the decades, have all paraded through the Brandenburger Tor, up the splendid tree-lined avenue, Unter den Linden, to the palace of Prussia's hereditary rulers, the Hohenzollerns.

The broad expanse in front of the gate used to be an elegant enclosed urban space, the *Quarre*, renamed **Pariser Platz** after the Wars of Liberation. With stately eighteenth-century palaces, this was the best address in Berlin. The sumptuous Hotel Adlon was here; so was the

Lenin in the Russian embassy

French embassy. Immediately to the right of the gate lived the Expressionist painter Max Liebermann. He directed visitors: "To find my house, enter Berlin and take the first left." Born into a prominent family of Berlin Jews in 1847, Liebermann encouraged a younger generation of modernist painters in Wilhelmine Germany, served as president of the Prussian Academy of Arts, and lived long enough to see the Nazis come to power. With the images of torch-bearing brownshirts on Pariser Platz in mind, Liebermann once remarked: "It is a pity I can't eat as much as I want to puke." Liebermann died in 1935, and his widow committed suicide just before the deportation of Berlin Jews began in 1942.

Napoleon rode through this gate for the first time on October 27, 1806, after Prussia's humiliating defeat at the battle of Jena. An eyewitness remembered that "in front of the Brandenburger Tor, Napoleon glanced up for a moment at the Goddess of Victory, commemorating the four victories of Prussia over his own nation. . . . The earnestness of his face is seldom broken by a smile; and yet he has a strange smile, quite peculiar to him, a smile that does not permit others to smile when they stand in his presence. I saw him smile like that once during the entry into Berlin, when he heard not only his own troops shouting '*Vive l'Empereur*' but also a large number of the Berliners themselves." Many Germans thought Napoleon's triumphal entry was their liberation from oppressive Hohenzollern absolutism.

After eight heavily taxed years, however, the loyalty of Berliners reverted to their king, and they celebrated the final defeat of France on August 7, 1814, with a victory parade that returned the *Quadriga*, the copper sculpture of Nike astride her chariot by Johann G. Schadow, to the top of Brandenburger Tor. Nike is the goddess of victory on the sports field as well as the battlefield, and she therefore honors national achievement as well as military conquest. In 1814, however, Schadow's Nike was given an additional cross to hold. The Iron Cross, an award for battlefield courage created especially for the Wars of Liberation, came to symbolize the German nation in arms. When East Germans returned the repaired *Quadriga* to the Brandenburger Tor in 1958, they were sensitive enough to first remove the

Quadriga *on the Bradenburger Tor*

Iron Cross; amid loud public debate the cross reappeared in August 1991.

Prussian soldiers slunk though the Brandenburger Tor and out of the city on March 21, 1848, after revolutionaries had occupied Berlin. Constitutional reform and German unification eluded the people, however. When representatives of the Frankfurt Parliament arrived in Berlin some months later, King Friedrich Wilhelm IV refused their offer to rule a unified German nation, not just the Prussian state. Their offer came not from God or the German princes but merely from the people—or from the "gutter" as he put it. On June 16, 1871, a German emperor finally did march through the Brandenburger Tor at the head of a tumultuous victory parade that lasted five hours; the king of Prussia had been crowned emperor (or kaiser) of Germany thanks to the victory of German arms on the battlefields of France.

The Brandenburger Tor was also the site of street fighting in the German Revolution of November 1918. The monarchy collapsed without so much as a whimper at the end of World War I. In the hardship weeks that followed, factions of right-wing soldiers, republicans, and socialists battled for position. Harry Graf

Kessler, the great diarist of the Weimar Republic, observed fighting in the very center of the capital on January 8, 1919: "The Wilhelmstrasse is impassable," he wrote. "A gun has been mounted in front of the Chancellory. At intervals a machine gun fires from the balcony of the Ministry of the Interior. . . . I made my way to the upper part of Unter den Linden. To the rat-tat-tat of distant machine guns, life proceeded almost normally. A fair amount of traffic, some shops and cafes open, street vendors peddling their wares, and barrel organs grinding away as usual. . . . At four o'clock I was in the Friedrichstrasse. There was a good deal of traffic. . . . Leipziger Strasse, except for its closed shops, looked perfectly normal, and the big cafes on Potsdamer Platz were open, brightly lit, and doing business as usual. . . . Single shots were dropping all the time. As I left about nine, street vendors with cigarettes, malt goodies, and soap were still crying their wares."

Hitler eventually extinguished this republican Germany. With his appointment as chancellor on January 30, 1933, brownshirted Nazis massed around the Brandenburger Tor. In his memoirs, *Fateful Years*, the diplomat André-François Poncet commented on looking out from the French embassy on Pariser Platz, to the right of the gate: "These torches form a single river of fire, and the waves of this swelling river build up to advance with great power into the heart of the capital. And from these men in brown shirts and high boots, marching in disciplined ranks and singing warlike songs as loudly as they can and as if with one voice, there comes a new enthusiasm, a dynamic force. The spectators are seized by this enthusiasm, and they break into long and continuous shouts which coincide with the pace of the march and the rhythm of the men singing."

Just beyond the Brandenburger Tor one can see the elegant neoclassical **Reichstag**, the German parliament building, completed in 1894, which is remembered more for what it failed to do than for what it achieved. The Reichstag never managed to gain full constitutional powers from the German kaisers or to put democracy on a stable footing in the 1920s or to prevent the rise of Hitler. When a lone Communist set fire to the Reichstag in February 1933 (as historians have now conclusively established), Hitler used the misdeed to assume dictatorial power. In recent years the Reichstag has stood mutely at the very side of the Berlin Wall. Only after 1989, with the demolition of the wall and the reunification of Germany, does it face a brighter future.

The new order that the Nazis hoped to impose very nearly destroyed Berlin. By 1945, much of Pariser Platz and Unter den Linden stood in ruins. The first great Allied bombing raid hit Berlin on the night of November 22, 1943. Hans-Georg von Studnitz wandered through the city the next morning: "Around the destroyed Alexanderplatz S-Bahn station, the big department stores are blazing. . . . In the city center, Schlüter's splendid castle . . . still stands in the middle of a great storm of smoke and sparks. Huge flames rise up out of one wing. . . . The armory, the university, Saint Hedwig's Cathedral, the 'Kommode,' and the National Library are already reduced to ashes. Clouds of smoke obscure the view from Unter den Linden into the Friedrichstrasse and Wilhelmstrasse. On the Pariser Platz, the IG Farben building is in flames. The Adlon, opposite, seems unharmed. The French embassy, the Friedländer Palais, the casino, the guardhouses built by Schinkel on either side of the Brandenburger Tor show for the last time the graceful lines of their design against the fiery background." The Soviets finally liberated Berlin and raised the hammer and sickle on top of the Brandenburger Tor on April 30, 1945.

After the war, the Brandenburger Tor stood right on the border between East and West Berlin. Until the wall was built in 1961, pedestrians were free to come and go, although border guards monitored traffic to make sure that East Berliners did not intend to flee or smuggle goods to the West. A wonderful Cold War anecdote has it that a man on a bicycle pedaled through the Brandenburger Tor. East German guards stopped and asked him what he had in his overfilled backpack. He replied: sand. The guards opened the pack, emptied and sifted through the sand, and gave the bicyclist permission to refill his bag and proceed. The next day he was back. Once again he had a backpack full of sand, which the guards carefully inspected without finding anything. For a week the man rode to the Brandenburger Tor. Each day he was stopped, checked, and then waved through. Finally, one of the guards went up to the man. "We know you are smuggling," he said, "but we don't know what." After being cleared one more time, the man laughed and answered: "Bicycles."

After the construction of the wall on August 13, 1961, the Brandenburger Tor stood in a dead border zone, inaccessible to the crowds of tourists who pressed against the border on either side. Surely one of the last people to expect the demolition of the Berlin Wall or an end to the Cold War was Ronald Reagan, who stood on the western side in the spring of 1987 and told the Soviets to "tear down this wall." However, East and West and all the certainties of the postwar world crumbled on the strange afternoon of November 9, 1989, when East German officials remarked that, yes, East Berliners were free to come and go. Over the course of that night, thousands of Berliners crossed through hastily constructed openings in the wall and celebrated the mobility they had been denied for twenty-eight years. It was nothing less than a media spectacle in front of the Brandenburger Tor, moderated by television anchors from around the world. Today, the ramshackle landscape from Potsdamer Platz to Pariser Platz cautions visitors against too much euphoria: The integration of eastern Germany is fraught with economic difficulty. The new government district of the Federal Republic to be built around here by the year 2000 faces its share of challenges and also offers opportunities in the new century.

The best way to leave Pariser Platz is to take bus #100 to Bahnhof Zoologischer Garten or back up Unter den Linden to Alexanderplatz.

Walk · 2

The Scheunenviertel

THE JEWISH QUARTER

Krausnickstrasse

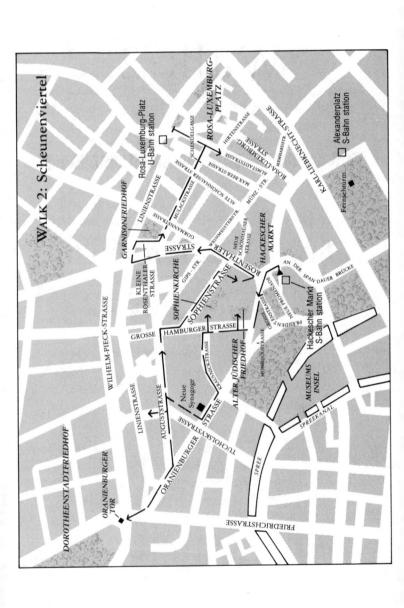

WALK 2: Scheunenviertel

Rosa-Luxemburg-Platz U-Bahn station

ROSA-LUXEMBURG-PLATZ

ROSA-LUXEMBURG-STRASSE

KARL-LIEBKNECHT-STRASSE

Alexanderplatz S-Bahn station

Fernsehturm

Schendelgasse

HIRTENSTRASSE

MAX-BEER-STRASSE

ALMSTADTSTRASSE

ALTE SCHÖNHAUSER STRASSE

MÜNZ. STR.

GARNISONFRIEDHOF

LINIENSTRASSE

GORMANNSTRASSE

MULACKSTRASSE

WILHELM-PIECK-STRASSE

KLEINE ROSENTHALER-STRASSE

GIPS- STR.

Sophienkirche

SOPHIENSTRASSE

STRASSE

ROSENTHALER

WEINMEISTERSTR.

NEUE SCHÖNHAUSER STRASSE

HACKESCHER MARKT

AN DER SPANDAUER BRÜCKE

GROSSE

HAMBURGER STRASSE

NEUE PROMENADE

PRÄSIDENTENSTRASSE

GROSSE PRÄSIDENTENSTR.

Hackescher Markt S-Bahn station

LINIENSTRASSE

AUGUSTSTRASSE

Neue Synagoge

KRAUSNICKSTRASSE

ALTER JÜDISCHER FRIEDHOF

MONBIJOUSTRASSE

MUSEUMS INSEL

DOROTHEENSTADTFRIEDHOF

ORANIENBURGER TOR

TUCHOLSKYSTRASSE

ORANIENBURGER STRASSE

SPREEKANAL

SPREE

FRIEDRICHSTRASSE

Starting Point: S-Bahn station Hackescher Markt
Transportation: S-Bahn to Hackescher Markt Station
Length: About 2 hours

Weekday afternoons are probably the best time to take this walk, and the Sophienkirche is open late on Wednesday afternoon.

The *Scheunenviertel* is one of Berlin's oldest surviving neighborhoods and, since reunification, one of Berlin's most lively. The district was initially established in the 1670s when the Great Elector Friedrich Wilhelm ordered fire hazards such as stables and storage sheds to be built outside the medieval city walls. The name of this area, Scheunenviertel, means stable district. In time, poor people erected hastily built shelters around these stables, giving the area a distinctly proletarian feel. But the neighborhood also has a three-hundred-year history of Jewish settlement, and it is with this history that the Scheunenviertel is most closely associated.

Our walk begins at Grosse Hamburger Strasse, an age-old road that led over Neuruppin, where both Schinkel and the novelist Theodor Fontane were born, to Hamburg. To get there, take the S-Bahn to Hackescher Markt. The brick station, which dates from 1882, is the only completely original S-Bahn station left in Berlin. At one end, a handsome Irish pub, **Kilkenny's**, has moved into the viaduct arches. With Guinness and more on tap, this is a welcoming and sunny spot that you might want to keep in mind when we briefly return to this area or when you need a break after visiting the nearby Museumsinsel. For our purposes, follow the signs to Hackescher Markt. As you leave the station, you are leaving behind the old fortifications that surrounded medieval Berlin. The street leading away from the station is still called **An der Spandauer Brücke**; a bridge once led over a defensive trench that had been dug just beyond the city walls. This is a good place to sit on a bench and consider the traces of history.

Eike Geisel, a young Berlin historian who was one of the first scholars to rediscover this district, wrote bitterly about the loss of history and particularly the loss of Jewish history. "Whoever searches for traces of the ghetto," he writes in his history, *lm Scheunenviertel*, "always ends up empty-handed. Nothing has remained except for the poverty of the houses. Every street of the quarter has unsightly gaps, every house is a social case in stone. Every gray and pockmarked façade is a gate that is closed to the past." A few faint traces of this world on the other side of World War II can still be found, but the sense of irretrievable loss hovers over these quiet streets. The Nazis cut the threads of continuity long ago.

Jewish immigrants have enriched the culture and prosperity of Berlin for hundreds of years. Along with the French Huguenots, they constitute one of the oldest communities in the metropolis. A Jüden Strasse behind the *Rotes Rathaus* on Alexanderplatz (Walk 3) indicates a Jewish presence already in the Middle Ages, but the historical beginning of the community dates from 1671 when the Great Elector offered fifty wealthy Jewish families from Vienna asylum in Berlin. They, like Austria's other Jews and Protestants, had been banished from the realm by the Catholic emperor Leopold I. The Hohenzollerns, on the other hand, were glad to put Jewish capital and skill to work and allowed the families to purchase land, conduct business, and privately practice their religion, although the Great Elector did not permit the erection of a synagogue. The cornerstone for the *Grossschul* synagogue was not laid until 1712. Once Jews received permission to settle in Berlin, however, they were required to purchase 400 taler of porcelain from the Royal Porcelain Factory. The factory did the selecting and thus unloaded all its old and badly manufactured stock on the Jews. They were forced to subsidize the king's own factories and were also prohibited from competing with the king's subjects. Throughout the eighteenth century, Jews could not practice any trade that was regulated by a guild.

Despite these restrictions and indignities, the Jewish community in Berlin prospered and felt itself an integral part of German cultural life. Moses Mendelssohn, who had arrived in Berlin in 1743 as an impoverished fourteen-year-old, worked closely with the bookseller Friedrich Nicolai and the writer Gotthold Lessing to further the ideas of German Enlightenment. At the beginning of the 1800s, Romantic intellectuals such as Friedrich von Schlegel, Friedrich Schleiermacher, E.T.A. Hoffmann, and the brothers Alexander and Wilhelm von Humboldt met in the literary salons of Henriette Herz and Rahel Varnhagen, who were both born into prominent Jewish families. But the Jewish community remained small, perhaps four thousand to five thousand members, until the middle of the nineteenth century. Berlin's explosive industrial growth attracted working-class immigrants, some of them Jews, from Poland and Russia as well as East Prussia and Silesia. Jews also fled pogroms in the Russian Empire in massive numbers. By the turn of the century, thousands of immigrants had transplanted their Eastern European

Jewish culture to the urban streets of the Scheunenviertel. At the same time, all sorts of Yiddish words—such as *meshugge* (crazy), *mies* (awful), and *pleite* (broke)—made their way into Berlin dialect. The Scheunenviertel proved to be no sanctuary, however, once the Nazi terror began. This district was the gathering site for the mass deportations of Berlin's Jews beginning in 1942.

The post–World War II years accelerated the prewar decay of the neighborhood. With its stock of dilapidated housing, the Scheunenviertel was targeted by the former East German government for urban renewal on a large scale. Fortunately, the Berlin Wall came down before all the historic buildings did. As you walk through this district, you will see many tenement buildings occupied by squatters as well as dozens of new shops, art galleries, and cafes. Many of East Berlin's artists claimed this area as their own in an attempt to ward off property speculation by West German developers. The district thus has its own flavor, a distinct blend of prewar heritage and East Berlin sensibility. Today, the Scheunenviertel is home to a renascent Jewish community—again welcoming Jews from East European countries—and a bustling young artistic community.

Now let's enter the Scheunenviertel itself. Walk along An der Spandauer Brücke toward the streetcar traffic and cross Neue Promenade, keeping the traffic circle on your right. Continue straight ahead and a bit to your left, and you will be facing Oranienburger Strasse. Turn left into Oranienburger Strasse (without taking the sharp left onto Grosse Präsidenten Strasse), a bustling street of galleries, stores, and workshops, and then take the first right into Grosse Hamburger Strasse. After a few yards, turn into the green park on your right. "Don't trust the green places," recommends Berlin observer Heinz Knobloch, and rightly so since this well-kept lawn was not always so peaceful. It covers the site of what was once the district's Jewish old-age home, a collection point for the deportation of Berlin Jews to the killing camps in 1942 and

Memorial to Berlin's Jewish Deportees

1943, and behind it the **Alter Jüdischer Friedhof**, the oldest Jewish cemetery in Berlin, laid out in 1671 and desecrated by the Nazis in 1942. Across the street, the half-timbered house at Grosse Hamburger Strasse 19 is almost as old as the cemetery; it first shows up in city records in 1695. As Berlin grew and new districts surrounded the old cemetery, the Jewish community purchased ground for a larger cemetery on the city outskirts. It opened in 1827 along Schönhauser Allee; we will pass it on Walk 3. In two generations, however, the press of working-class neighborhoods enveloped that site as well. It was closed and replaced in 1880 by the huge cemetery in Weissensee, the largest Jewish cemetery in central Europe. The movement of the Jewish cemeteries thus traces the tumultuous growth of nineteenth-century Berlin.

Enter this parklike cemetery along the wide path. Before 1945 the entrance was a narrow corridor to the left of the Jewish old-age home, which was destroyed in the last year of the war. The old-age home was founded in 1829 but was taken over by the *Gestapo* (security police) in 1942 and turned into a collection point for the deportation of Berlin's 56,000 remaining Jews (down from 160,000 in 1933); for them, Grosse Hamburger Strasse 26 became synonymous with National Socialist terror. One chronicler of the deportation wrote, "At this place, which was once erected for the preservation of life, thousands of Jewish people were assembled and prepared for destruction and death. The building was turned into a prison, fitted with bars on the windows, and guarded by sentries on the street and at the entrance. Huge searchlights lit up the front and the back." The very last of the 63 deportation transports left Berlin in early April 1945.

Infants, grandparents, World War I veterans, and other ordinary Berliners were all readied for transport to Auschwitz or other concentration camps under the eyes of their non-Jewish neighbors. As you can see, apartment houses surround the cemetery, offering unhindered views of this site of horror. Berlin writer Lutz Rathenow once struck up a conversation with an old woman in the Scheunenviertel who remembered some of her Jewish neighbors. When questioned about the deportations, however, she told stories about the war, about how an incendiary bomb fell through the roof and into the kitchen, where it landed on a bowl of herring. The bomb was a dud, but the fish had to be thrown away, she recalled. Memory takes strange records and leaves wide gaps.

Today, the former cemetery is a quiet green park that invites reflection and remembrance. This cemetery once contained three thousand simple gravestones; almost all were demolished by the Nazis, although a few remnants can be found in the south wall. A new gravestone has been erected for Moses Mendelssohn (1729–1786), the prominent Enlightenment philosopher and friend of Berlin intellectuals such as Gotthold Lessing who made "Herr Moses" the model for his drama *Nathan the Wise*.

As you leave the cemetery, the same way you came in, take a look at Will and Mark Lammer's stark group statue (1985) that commemorates the deported Jews on the site of the former old-age home. Following Jewish practice, visitors have put small stones of remembrance on the nearby memorial plaque. A service is held here every February 27, the anniversary of the 1943 *Fabrikation*, the final wave of large-scale deportations that rounded up Berlin's last thousand Jews working in war industries.

The handsome building to the left of the cemetery at #27 is the old Jewish boys' school; above the portal an inscription still reads *Knabenschule der jüdischen Gemeinde*. It reopened in August 1992 as a Jewish grammar school after having been closed by the Nazis exactly fifty years earlier. It was Mendelssohn who founded the school in 1778. Enlightenment figure that he was, Mendelssohn wanted to break down the religious barriers that for centuries imposed isolation on the Jewish community. He envisioned an institution that would teach secular subjects as well as Jewish tradition, and for a time, at the beginning of the nineteenth century, the well-regarded school even opened its doors to non-Jewish pupils. The school moved to its present site on Grosse Hamburger Strasse in 1863, and the present building was erected in 1906. A bust of the famous philosopher was unveiled in front of the school in February 1909. Nazi toughs shattered the sculpture in 1941, but a new Mendelssohn bust now stands in the courtyard of West Berlin's Jewish community (Fasenenstrasse 79–80), though a plaque here remembers Moses Mendelssohn's quotable words: *Nach Wahrheit forschen, Schönheit lieben, Gutes wollen, das Beste tun.* (Search for truth, love beauty, desire virtue, do the best.)

Directly across the street, at Grosse Hamburger Strasse 15–16, is an impressive piece of urban art, *The Missing House*, which was conceived in 1990 by Christian Boltanski as part of the citywide exhibition *Die Endlichkeit der Freiheit.* (The title is a play on words and suggests the Final Arrival of Freedom as well as the Finite Limits to Freedom.) Boltanski used the empty lot to recall the autobiographies of the residents of the building that was completely destroyed by a bomb just before noon on February 3, 1945. Signs on each of the adjacent walls name some of the former residents, many of whom were Jewish, and indicate the sociology of the neighborhood. You can see that a hairdresser, a police assistant, and a piano teacher lived here. Unfortunately, the archival records and family photographs that the intrepid Boltanksi gathered have been dispersed and are no longer on view. Nonetheless, this gap in the street has filled in many gaps in historical memory. A small booklet (in German) on the exhibition can be purchased in the Heimat Museum around the corner at Sophienstrasse 23.

Allied bombing raids created empty lots like this one throughout Berlin. Residents who lived in adjacent back courtyards suddenly had light, and their damp apartments dried out; local wits joked that these poor people were World War II's *Kriegsgewinnler*, or war profiteers. This black wartime humor also renamed the bombed-out Charlottenburg neighborhood *Klamottenburg* (*Klamotten* are old clothes) and Steglitz, *Steht nichts* (Nothing Left).

Back across Grosse Hamburger Strasse, a few paces from the school, right next to the inviting antiquarian bookstore *Goethe & Co* (at #28), is the courtyard in front of the **Sophienkirche**, the only surviving baroque church in Berlin. It was erected to serve the growing community of poor people beyond the city's medieval walls. Queen Sophie Luise was the church's major benefactor, having donated 4,000 taler, a substantial sum at the time; the cornerstone was laid in 1712, although the tower was not completed until 1734. The property was not quite large enough, however, and the Jewish community, anxious to build good relations, readily donated a section of its cemetery, asking in return only that the congregation teach its children to respect their Jewish neighbors. Since then, Grosse Hamburger Strasse has been known *im Volksmund* (literally, in the mouth of the people) as Tolerance Street—tolerant because of the unusual circumstances that brought together in peaceful coexistence a

Sophienkirche

Protestant congregation, a Jewish community, and, farther up the street, a Catholic hospital, Saint Hedwig's, which opened in 1854. Tolerant also because of the liberal spirit that prevailed. Mendelssohn's boys' school, for example, welcomed non-Jewish students and taught secular subjects. The Sophienkirche protected East Germany's small peace movement and, beginning in 1975, long before memorials were placed on Grosse Hamburger Strasse, sponsored Jewish-Christian discussion groups. And Saint Hedwig Hospital treated Jewish and Protestant as well as Catholic patients.

It is ironic that Leopold von Ranke (1795–1886), the scholar who claimed to write "history as it actually was," is buried in a family grave in the small Sophienkirche cemetery—ironic because the very idea of a correct version of history seems very much in doubt when applied to the Scheunenviertel. The area has seen such wrenching changes, has been the scene of so many different kinds of stories—about Germans and Jews, for example—and has buried much of the past either through forgetfulness, willful destruction, or simply repression. The Scheunenviertel suggests that history is an arabesque rather than a straight line, a pattern to be rediscovered again and again rather than a story told once and for all. Goethe's friend Carl Friedrich Zelter (1758–1832), who appears so often in the great writer's letters and essays, lies here as well. The church is open on Wednesday afternoon from 4 to 6.

More than two years after the deportation of most of Berlin's Jews, World War II drew to a close in these narrow streets. Most of the fighting for Berlin in April 1945 occurred in the eastern suburbs, on Frankfurter Strasse, along which the Russians advanced, and around the Reichstag. But Soviet and German tanks battled in the Scheunenviertel as well, and buildings are scarred with shell fragments and machine-gun fire. As this district is gradually renovated, new sandstone façades will inevitably cover the stark remembrances of world war in the city. To inspire memories, a metal frame on which "Pax" is written was placed around one scarred section of the façade at Grosse Hamburger Strasse 29 in 1987; the effect is quite moving.

Theodor Fontane, whose melancholy novels about Prussia at the close of the nineteenth century—*Der Stechlin*, *Effi Briest*, and *Delusions, Confusions*—remain masterpieces, lived at **Grosse Hamburger Strasse 30–30a** with his aunt and uncle in the 1830s. He remembered the cold winters; his room was so damp, he wrote afterward, "that water ran in great rivulets down the walls." Farther up the street, at #35, you can watch an artisan skillfully create guitars, mandolins, cellos, and violins; this is one of many handsome workshops and ateliers that have established themselves in the Scheuenviertel.

Turn left into **Krausnickstrasse**, directly across from the front courtyard of the Sophienkirche. The street is named for a largely forgotten Berlin mayor, but it recalls the atmosphere of a typical working-class neighborhood in the nineteenth century. As you make your way along this street, you'll see more of the shell- and shrapnel-scarred façades. Years of neglect are slowly being repaired, but for the time being one can still see prewar storefront advertising over abandoned shops. In the summer, bright geraniums in window boxes help relieve the gray monotony. You should know that Berliners take their flowers very seriously. They are tended with great care on dilapidated windowsills, on the balconies that grace older buildings, and in small garden patches (*Laubenkolonien*) that are cultivated throughout the city.

At the end of the block, turn right onto Oranienburger Strasse; you might want to cross to the far side of the street to better see the **New Synagogue**, which is in the middle of the block. Built in 1866, the New Synagogue is the oldest surviving synagogue in Berlin; it was called *new* only to distinguish it from the vanished *old* eighteenth-century *Grossschul* that was near the S-Bahn station Hackescher Markt at the southern edge of the present-day Scheunenviertel. Long a neglected ruin, the New Synagogue is being beautifully restored in the early 1990s and ranks once again among the great landmarks of the city.

In the two centuries after the original settlement of fifty Viennese families, Berlin's Jewish community thrived. Approximately twenty-eight thousand Jews made up some 4 percent of the city's population in 1866, and it was these growing numbers that the New Synagogue was meant to serve. The monumental size of the building, designed by Eduard Knoblauch, a Christian, and its placement right on the street make the synagogue immediately recognizable as a Jewish house of worship. Imbibing the optimistic spirit of the liberal age, Berlin's Jews saw no reason to hide their synagogue as had formerly been the custom. Indeed, the 160-foot-high dome did not, as was first intended, crown the actual synagogue, which was diagonally set back from the street where there was more room, but the street-front foyer. The New Synagogue proclaimed a proud tradition of service to and economic cooperation with the city and the Prussian state. And the Jewish community looked forward to the future in a spirit of unabashed assimilation. The pronounced Islamic style of the building, with its turrets and traceries, not only recalls a golden age of Jewish culture in Moorish Spain but proclaims as well a Jewish renaissance in nineteenth-century Prussia. Exposed bands of colored brick and terra-cotta decoration also reveal the strong influence of Schinkel, who was Knoblauch's teacher. The Hebrew inscription over the entrance reads: "Open the gates to let a righteous nation in, a nation that keeps faith."

While the exterior of the synagogue recalled Moorish Spain, many aspects of the congregation's service incorporated Christian customs. The synagogue, which seated three thousand worshipers, featured one of Berlin's largest organs, a mixed choir, and German-language services but notably excluded ritual baths. According to Baedeker, a "dim religious light from the stained glass and the cupolas produces a remarkably fine effect." Even public concerts, including one by the violinist and Nobel Prize–winning physicist Albert Einstein on September 29, 1930, were held in the marvelous synagogue. These innovations of Reform Judaism eventually divided the congregation, however; in 1869, more orthodox members established their own synagogue and cultural center, which we will see farther on.

With Bismarck and other ranking Prussian officials in attendance, the New Synagogue was dedicated on September 5, 1866, just a few days before the triumphal return to the city of Prussian troops who had defeated Austria and thereby cleared the way for Prussia's unification of the other German states. It was the beginning of German statehood, with which Berlin Jews wholly identified. The community around the New Synagogue felt itself German to the core and actively supported the national cause of Germany. At the same time, however, an increasingly chauvinistic nationalism attempted to segregate Jews from other Germans. This was a sharp challenge to the liberal spirit that had built the New Synagogue and a reminder that Moorish Spain, too, had been vanquished in 1492 by the Catholic *Reconquista*, which banished Spain's Moslems and Jews.

In the 1880s, the Berlin historian Heinrich von Treitschke lamented the supposedly overweening influence of the Jews in German life, influence to which the grandeur of the New Synagogue evidently attested. Moreover, Treitschke claimed that the building's Moorish style underscored the alien nature of Germany's Jews. Even though the proportion of Jews in Berlin's fast-growing population continued to hover around 4 percent, attacks on Jews, particularly in the Scheunenviertel, mounted in the late nineteenth century. Confidence in assimilationism frayed, and synagogues built later, such as the one on Rykestrasse in Prenzlauer Berg (which we will see on Walk 3), were designed in a less ostentatious fashion.

The New Synagogue was an obvious target in the Nazi pogrom on the night of November 9–10, 1938, known as *Kristallnacht*. Here as elsewhere in Germany, synagogues were burned, stores looted, and Jews attacked and arrested. The interior of the New Synagogue was wrecked by brownshirted Nazis, who also beat up Jewish residents and smashed the storefronts of Jewish-owned stores. The morning after *Kristallnacht* (or crystal night, so-named for the shards of broken glass that littered the streets), a young child from the district, Ruth Gross, recounted in her memoirs how all at once "neighbors became Jews," a phrase she later used to title her memoirs. She walked with her father up Oranienburger Strasse. "Glass shards, Bibles, and prayer books lay in heaps on the sidewalk," she recalled. "I wanted to pick up one of the holy books since it is a sin to throw them in the dirt, but my father pulled me back with a frightened start. I couldn't understand this—I was seven years old then. . . . He knew the danger that surrounded us; I only slowly came to realize it." Most non-Jewish neighbors averted their eyes altogether. As the synagogue burned, nurses just down the street at Saint Hedwig's Hospital were admonished not to look out the window: "Don't make yourself a witness," they were told. Both the pogrom and the silence of non-Jewish neighbors cleared the way for harsher measures: the "Aryanization" of Jewish businesses; the banishment of Jews from public life; the requirement to wear the yellow star; and, after 1942, deportation and extermination.

It has long been assumed that when the Nazis set fire to the synagogue on November 9, 1938, the building was completely gutted. (A famous period photograph shows the synagogue seemingly engulfed in flames.) But historical records mention Sabbath services held in the New Synagogue in 1939, and a report on 1943 bomb damage to an army warehouse bears the address of the (requisitioned) synagogue: Oranienburger Strasse 29–30. Moreover, a number of memoirists recall the synagogue's being saved in 1938 by a police lieutenant, who was said to have been hanged at the end of the war by the Nazis for his courageous deed.

A local journalist, Heinz Knobloch, finally tracked down the real story. Relying on the account of Hans Hirschberg, a Jew born in Berlin and now living in Israel, Knobloch wrote a magazine piece about the unknown police lieutenant who arrived just in time at the New Synagogue with official documents that proved the building had been designated an architectural landmark fifty years earlier. The Gestapo thereupon retreated and allowed firemen to extinguish the blaze.

Since the local police precinct on Rosenthaler Strasse, across from the *Hackesche Höfe*, had long since disappeared, Knobloch asked his readers for information. Knobloch eventually received a letter from the son of the unknown lieutenant. As it turned out, the police lieutenant, Wilhelm Krützfeld, was not a socialist or a committed anti-fascist but simply a civil servant with a strong sense of right and wrong. As head of the precinct at Hackescher Markt, he helped and warned persecuted neighborhood Jews numerous times. Krützfeld was severely reprimanded after saving the synagogue and retired anonymously rather than enforce deportations in 1942. He died peacefully in 1953. One mystery that Knobloch was not able to unravel: the origin of the photograph that shows the synagogue in flames in 1938 when in fact it burned as a result of fierce British air raids on November 22, 1943. In any case, the restored New Synagogue will not revert to its religious function (the congregation hall was razed in the 1950s) but will serve as the centerpiece of the *Centrum Judaicum*, scheduled to open in 1995.

Flanking the New Synagogue are buildings that once belonged and now have been returned to the Jewish community. On the left, at **#31**, is the former Jewish Museum, which opened on an inauspicious January 24, 1933, only six days before Hitler assumed power. It was completely ransacked by the Nazis on Kristallnacht. The **Jüdische Gallerei Berlin** now displays a nice collection of art at this location (gallery hours are Monday through Friday, 10 am to 6:30 pm; Sunday, 12 pm to 3 pm). On the other side of the synagogue, at **#28**, are the administrative offices of the Jewish community. During World War II, the Nazis located in this building the Reich Genealogical Office, the bureau charged with investigating the racial origins of Germans. Years of neglect followed, and only recently has the building been restored. At #28 you will also find **Oren**, a very popular restaurant that serves some traditional Jewish food, German regional dishes, and Radeberger beer, a famous brew from Dresden. In the foyer to Oren there are listings of cultural and intellectual events of interest to the Jewish community.

At the end of the block, at the corner of Oranienburger and Tucholskystrasse, is a massive orange building that seems to compete with the synagogue for your attention. This is the old **Postfuhramt**, a post office depot, one of the first official structures built (1875–81) after Berlin had become the capital of the German Reich in 1871. Berlin's superintendent of buildings, Hermann Blankenstein, felt that a state building could not be overshadowed by a synagogue, even if its functions were rather prosaic: The Postfuhramt warehoused postal carriages and carts and stabled some 240 horses. The handsome brickwork and terra-cotta adornments recall the characteristic style that Schinkel sought for Berlin, but the building's colossal proportions also anticipate the gaudy post–1888 imperial style of Wilhelm II, for whom everything had to be grand, imposing, and sumptuous, like the Berliner Dom on the Lustgarten (Walk 1). For all the grandeur here, though, the post office quickly dispensed with horses in an age of automobiles; the last hooves clattered out of the cobblestoned courtyard in 1925.

Turn back toward the New Synagogue and enter the interesting series of courtyards behind the building at **Oranienburger Strasse 32**. The doors may be closed, but it is perfectly all right to enter this behind-the-scenes passageway. In the first courtyard a series of low stables once provided carriage houses and living quarters for Berlin coachmen; the rooms above these rickety stables are still inhabited. The bust of a horse's head peacefully gazes out from the other side of the courtyard. Farther along, the metalwork of a modern-day sculptor can be seen in the second courtyard. The ruin of an old cellar bar, *Zur Unterirdischen Tante*, or the Underground Aunt (the name is taken from an Ackerstrasse bar in a well-known Berlin novel by Edmund Graeser), reposes in a far corner of the third courtyard. The fading stenciling on the wall announces potato pancakes every Tuesday. It is hard to imagine that metropolitan interiors such as these were once packed with workshops, small businesses, and taverns, but before 1945 the ubiquitous Berlin courtyards were spaces for work, living, and entertainment. Now they are often stage sets for the East Berlin "scene." As you can see in the third courtyard, they are filled with spontaneous art pieces, sculptures, and the remnants of raucous performances. Artists have also established their workshops on the ground floor of abandoned factories.

Now let's exit the courtyards at Auguststrasse 16; turn left and walk the few steps to the corner of Tucholskystrasse. Most of the buildings visible from this corner date from the period 1830 to 1850. These grim structures are among the first generation of *Mietskasernen*, a term that means rental barracks or simply tenements; they were erected for the growing proletarian population of industrial Berlin. The Borsig Machine Works, which built Germany's first steam locomotives, was established not far from here in 1837, among the factories in *Feuerland* (fire land), just outside Oranienburger Tor, and many Borsig workers lived in these impoverished dwellings.

Cross Tucholskystrasse and continue down Auguststrasse toward **Tacheles**, the large landmark ruin directly ahead of you that is now an alternative center for the arts. *Tacheles*, which comes from the Yiddish word that means "let's get down to business," is a warren of galleries, float-ing exhibits, cafes, and nightclubs. This has become a major landmark of the East Berlin "scene." On summer evenings thousands of young people have been known to crowd Oranienburger Strasse, blocking automobiles and streetcars and confirming just how much the gritty East, rather than the stylish West, now has the drawing power. Tacheles is not simply a wartime ruin but is in its own way a monument to the transitory nature of met-ropolitan Berlin.

Tacheles's first incarnation, just after the turn of the century, was as one of the cosmopolitan iron-and-glass arcades that fascinated writers such as Charles Baudelaire and Walter Benjamin. At the turn of the century, Oran-ienburger Strasse was a busy commercial thoroughfare. In the surrounding streets, hundreds of retailers supplied the varied needs of this densely populated neighbor-hood. Two main train stations, Stettiner and Friedrich-strasse, were located near here as well. Developers thusp saw Oranienburger Tor as a lucrative location for an op-ulent department store with more than one hundred spe-cialty shops.

Opened to the public in the fall of 1909, this huge five-storied arcade—one of the last of this grand type ever built—connected Oranienburger with Friedrichstrasse. The building featured reinforced concrete walls and a soaring cupola. In addition to ten staircases, there were eleven passenger elevators, ten freight elevators, and six spiral chutes that transported packages to the basement for wrapping and shipping. Unfortunately, the arcade bankrupted its developers, who had mistaken Scheunen-viertel bustle for midtown prosperity.

After World War I, Germany's General Electric Com-pany turned the impressive structure into a "house of technology," where it exhibited electrical products and futuristic designs. The Nazis celebrated the technological innovations of the building as well, but it never found its proper place in metropolitan Berlin. Air raids heavily

Tacheles

damaged the structure in 1944, and the building continued to fall apart slowly; by 1989 only this small wing
remained standing on Oranienburger Strasse. It is now
protected as an architectural landmark.

Although originally slated for demolition, the building
was occupied in February 1990 by artists as part of a
wave of squatter actions. The 1989 revolution not only
created the opportunity to circumvent the previously
censurious East German regime but prompted an enormous outpouring of creative energy and artistic experimentation. A long-delayed intellectual confrontation with
East German state socialism took place in dozens of un-

likely places like Tacheles. At the same time, the prospect of reunification with wealthy West Germans raised fears that neighborhood rents would explode and that East German artists would be completely engulfed and their neighborhood habitats destroyed. The occupation of Tacheles and other buildings in the Scheunenviertel and in Prenzlauer Berg was thus a result of a variety of political and economic factors. For the most part, squatters have now reached rental agreements with the city and other owners. However intimidating Tacheles might appear, it is completely safe, puts on noteworthy exhibitions, and sponsors independent music in the evening. It is certainly worth a closer look. With Tacheles and, across the street, **Obst und Gemüse**, a popular bar that simply moved into an old state-run fruit and vegetable store and didn't change the now classic East German sign, Oranienburger Strasse is a new center of Berlin nightlife, replacing, in many respects, the "alternative" scene in the West Berlin neighborhood of Kreuzberg.

At Tacheles, Auguststrasse joins Oranienburger Strasse. If you wish, walk to the right (as you face Tacheles) down Oranienburger Strasse to the busy intersection with Friedrichstrasse. This was the site of the Oranienburger Tor, one of the fifteen tollgates of eighteenth-century Berlin. The intersection in the 1990s looks a lot like it did in the 1890s when it was known as *die bunte Ecke*, the colorful corner around which cabarets, variety theaters, and *Tingel-Tangel* attracted a metropolitan mix of Scheunenviertel characters, prostitutes, students from the Friedrich-Wilhelm University, and doctors from Berlin's general hospital. Before 1990, however, this area was dimly lit and almost completely lifeless; a half-dozen shops, most of which did not survive reunification, and a lonesome snack bar hardly deserved a second glance. Now the entire region around Oranienburger Strasse is flourishing. But the neighborhood has also become unfamiliar to old-time residents who must deal with new urban problems such as petty crime, street noise, and prostitution. At the bunte Ecke today there are no galleries or luxury shops but plenty of retailers, hustlers, and curbside traffic. Perhaps the Scheunenviertel of old is not so far away after all.

Now we're going to go back up Auguststrasse and turn left at Tucholskystrasse, which is named for Kurt Tucholsky, the Weimar-era satirist. The center of the Orthodox Jewish community, **Adass Yisroel**, is located at Tucholskystrasse 40. Founded in 1869 in reaction to the reformism of the New Synagogue on Oranienburger Strasse, Adass Yisroel moved to its present location in 1904, was forcibly disbanded by the Nazis in 1939, and after fifty years was reestablished here in 1989. Six ritual baths and a synagogue can accommodate eight hundred worshipers. A look through the cast-iron gate reveals an art nouveau–style portal. You will probably also see a policeman: Adass Yisroel, like all Jewish institutions in Berlin, is protected around the clock. The Orthodox congregation runs the small kosher **Beth Cafe** next door and **Kolbo**, a kosher store that opened around the corner at Auguststrasse 78 in April 1992. (Both close early on Friday in observance of the Sabbath.) As Jewish life returns to the Scheunenviertel, new Jewish immigrants are arriving as well; Adass Yisroel actively helps many Soviet Jews who have elected to immigrate to Germany.

From Adass Yisroel look back down Tucholskystrasse. The *Hochschule für Jüdische Wissenschaften*, a Jewish seminary, once stood at the other end of the street (at #9, on the other side of Oranienburger Strasse). Berlin's reform rabbis were trained there, including a female rabbi in 1932 and Leo Baeck, the chief rabbi of Berlin's Jewish community in its most difficult years after 1933. Franz Kafka also attended lectures at the Hochschule in 1922.

With the Reform Jews down at one end of the street (which was called Artillerie Strasse before the war) and the Orthodox Jews at the other, the Berlin joke went, you had the advantage of both the light and the heavy artillery. It is amazing just how many sights in Berlin can be translated into military jargon. "In no other city will you find so many streets and squares named for battles and generals as in Berlin," reflected Viennese journalist Daniel Spitzer in 1880: "You will even find a street or squares dedicated to each kind of weapon."

Go back to the corner of Tucholskystrasse and Auguststrasse, then cross, and turn left onto Auguststrasse. You are now walking away from Tacheles. Head up the street and turn into the courtyard at **#14–15**. Ahead of you and wrapped around the left side of the courtyard is a building that once housed the **Hospital of the Jewish Community**. Completed in 1861, the hospital remained in use until 1914, after which it housed Jewish welfare agencies that worked desperately in the late 1930s to send Jewish children to Palestine. In 1942–43 it also served the Nazis as a collection point for Jews. On the right side is the **Bertolt Brecht Grammar School**, built in 1928 in Bauhaus style as a Jewish girls' school. Although the building's Jewish past has all but disappeared, traces of the more recent past can still be seen: The courtyard entryway features East German murals of "young pioneers" in the traditional uniform—white blouses and blue scarves. As you exit the courtyard onto Auguststrasse, note the building across the street at **#69**; it dates from the 1790s and is one of the oldest apartment buildings existent in Berlin. The faded sign MARGARINE FACTORY appears to be as old as the house itself but probably dates only from the 1940s. In the seventeenth and eighteenth centuries, Berlin's gallows stood on this site and gave Auguststrasse its original name: Armesündergasse, or Poor Sinners Lane.

Turn right to continue along Auguststrasse. The next stop is at #25, **Clärchens Ballhaus**, a Berlin original. This neighborhood dance hall is one of many that flourished in Berlin before and after World War I, but it is one of the very few that have survived the intervening decades of war, state socialism, and rock 'n' roll. The music played is sentimental, the clientele is mostly middle-aged, and each Wednesday features a "widow's ball"—ladies' choice. Clärchens opens at 7:30 pm every Tuesday through Saturday.

Another Berlin institution has survived next door at #26, **Druckerei Graetz**, a print shop founded in 1898 that is known for having printed many of Käthe Kollwitz's lithographs. Kollwitz (1867–1945) belongs to a generation of artists who made their name in the exhibitions of the Berlin Secession after the turn of the century. Unlike German Expressionists such as Ludwig Meidner, Ernst Ludwig Kirchner, and Otto Dix, Kollwitz did not execute grand canvases of metropolitan sights but cut finely observed prints of women and children and the private hardships of war, hunger, and sickness. (Kollwitz, who lived in Prenzlauer Berg, will be discussed more thoroughly in Walk 3.)

At the intersection of Auguststrasse and Grosse Hamburger Strasse, turn right and after a few yards turn left onto **Sophienstrasse**, one of the few examples of East German restoration. It had been typical of the regime to designate one street in a neighborhood to be expertly restored while the surrounding district was razed. As a result, several streets—looking almost like film sets—were carefully prepared for Berlin's *Jubiläum*, the city's 750th anniversary in 1987, and are scattered around former East Berlin: the Nicolai Quarter along the Spree; Husemannstrasse in Prenzlauer Berg, which we will pass on Walk 3; and Sophienstrasse in the Scheunenviertel.

Unlike the Nicolai Quarter, Sophienstrasse has been restored rather than recreated. What is more, the splendid eighteenth-century grace still retains a neighborhood feel. Although summer weekends bring numerous sightseers, at the end of an ordinary workday, mothers and fathers can be seen picking children up from school or buying groceries or chatting with neighbors. Cut-iron signs, evoking old guild signatures, hang by the storefronts, and stenciled advertising alerts customers to the wares and crafts found inside. Specialty shops abound here, but they share the street with more mundane retailers. For example, at the far end of the street, at #5, a charming shop specializing in wooden toys and jewelry faces a business selling plumbing supplies. The plumber, though, has good taste in window display.

As you wander down this street, you'll want to cross back and forth as storefronts catch your eye. We'll mention a few in particular, but first, if you are in need of refreshment, at the corner of Grosse Hamburger Strasse and Sophienstrasse, the **Sophien-Eck** offers drinks, snacks, and ice cream desserts in a lovely art nouveau setting; in the summer you can sit at outdoor tables at the corner or around back next to the Sophien Church grounds.

The Scheunenviertel's **Heimat Museum** is at **#23**, and a gallery is tucked into the peaceful courtyard at **#24**. To see just how urbane life in the city can be, peek into the remarkably inviting courtyard at **#22a**; look also at the beautifully restored art nouveau staircase inside the entrance on the left.

Across from the small church cemetery, enter the handsome brick building at **#18**, former home of the **Berliner Handwerkerverein**, or artisans' association, one of the first socialist organizations in Germany. The club was founded in 1844, and although it initially tried to alleviate the plight of master artisans and apprentices, it eventually became a thoroughly proletarian association, looking after the interests of the growing numbers of factory workers rather than of skilled guildsmen. A contemporary journalist described the first meetings in the hungry years of the 1840s: "Three or four hundred workers sat scattered among the tables to listen to lectures about their common interests and to participate in the discussion. The gatherings are opened with a club song, and the pauses between lectures are filled with song as well." The songs interspersing the lectures expressed the group's need for conviviality as well as politics.

In 1864 the club moved to this location on Sophien-strasse, and it was here that the newly unified Social Democratic Party of Germany held an early congress on December 15, 1874. For more than a century the So-cial Democratic Party—which is Germany's oldest party— has fought consistently for social reform and political democracy, and has nurtured outstanding German lead-ers, including Berlin's onetime mayor, the late Willy Brandt. The present building was erected in 1905 and hosted further revolutionary activities: This was also the site of early gatherings of the Communist Party, which split in 1919 from the more moderate Social Democrats in order to march in lockstep with the Russian Bolsheviks. A commemorative plaque also remembers the slave la-borers who were exploited in the building during World War II.

Continue down the right-hand side of the street to Sophienstrasse 6, and turn right into the narrow passage-way along the Sophien-Club, an inviting jazz bar and cultural center. You will find yourself in the **Hackesche Höfe**, an outstanding example of the courtyard culture that existed throughout Berlin. This was an enclosed working-class district of factories, offices, and some eighty apartments built in 1906–7 around nine courtyards. Originally, each courtyard had a different industrial func-tion and was appropriately adorned. Years of neglect and economic stagnation have left the courtyards, which sur-vived the war intact, shabby and undistinguished. Unless buildings are heated and maintained, the handsome glazed tiles crack and eventually fall off. Only the last of the courtyards, with its dark blue art nouveau tiling, re-calls the former glory of the Hackesche Höfe.

To wind your way through this complex, bear left along the main drive through the Höfe. The courtyards are accessed by alternate drives or connecting arches. You'll have to double back out of each to continue on your way. As you pass through the courtyards, imagine the noises and smells and sights of this industrial com-munity. The mix of factories and apartments right in the inner city is typical of Berlin; today, hundreds of small workshops and newly founded computer companies operate out of interior residential courtyards. (We will pass by more of these on Walk 4 through Kreuzberg.) In the last courtyard, look up at the second floor to see the beautiful tiling and the remains of the Imperial Dance Hall, a well-known nightclub from the 1920s. Today, on the right side, the cabaret **Varieté Chamäleon** is reviving the traditions of this unique urban space.

To exit, walk down along the courtyard entryway and turn left onto Rosenthaler Strasse. You are now back where you started, with the S-Bahn station Hackescher Markt on your right. As you start along Rosenthaler Strasse, glance into **#39**. The end of the small, narrow courtyard would not be worth a tourist's second look except that on this site one of the remarkable stories of the German resistance to Hitler took place. Otto Weidt operated his workshop for the blind, manufacturing brooms and brushes in a side building. During World War II, Weidt took in many blind Jews, providing them with employment, money, and ration cards, and even outfitted them with false papers. Nearly completely blind himself (or not so blind at all), Otto Weidt was a typical neighborhood operator. He traded and hoarded, bribed the Gestapo, and almost managed to save his employees. During the months of Nazi-organized deportations of Berlin's Jews, Weidt would go to the Gestapo and reclaim his Jewish workers, arguing that his workshop manufactured necessary war materials; indeed, Weidt had a contract with the army for brooms and brushes. In the end, however, the deportations netted even the last thousands of Jews working in war industries. On February 27 and 28, 1943, Weidt's blind workers were deported to Auschwitz. One of the workers survived, and Inge Deutschkron recalls Weidt and his efforts in her book, *Ich trug den gelben Stern* (*I Wore the Yellow Star*).

Rosenthaler Strasse has become a busy street with an attractive mix of stores, workshops, and cafes that en-

Art nouveau stairwell

chants the urban stroller, but the hurly-burly scene of clanging streetcars, billiard halls, cheap bars, pea soup at Aschinger's, and street vendors selling ties or pornography or pretzels that Alfred Döblin described in his novel *Berlin Alexanderplatz* is long gone. This was once the gritty metropolitan neighborhood stalked by Franz Biberkopf—ex-con, pimp, and anti-Semite, the Berliner at the center of Döblin's 1929 big-city epic. A few touches of old Berlin can be found, however. The building at the end of the courtyard, Rosenthaler Strasse 38, housed the Central Committee of the struggling Communist Party of Germany from 1921 to 1926. Next door, at **#37** and at **#36**, you can peek into the entrances to see the faded glory of magnificent art nouveau spiral staircases.

It is just a few more steps to Sophienstrasse. At this point, cross over to the other side of Rosenthaler Strasse. There on the corner (Rosenthaler and Neue Schönhauser Strasse) is the unassuming **Berolina Apotheke**, a pharmacy whose impressive dark-wood interior dates from 1887. Farther along Rosenthaler Strasse, at #51, is the newly opened and very comfortable **Cafe Paz**, a literary hangout. The second-floor establishment is open from 7 pm to 1 am.

Continue along the right-hand side of Rosenthaler Strasse, bearing slightly to the left with the curve of the street, and cross Weinmeister Strasse, ignoring for the time being the small offshoot misleadingly signposted Rosenthaler Strasse (it is actually called Kleine Rosenthaler Strasse). Pass Auguststrasse and turn right at the larger intersection with Linienstrasse. Once having run along the municipal border of the eighteenth-century city, Linienstrasse is lined with the solid but graceless concrete buildings that would have eventually replaced all the old tenements of the Scheunenviertel had it not been for the Revolution of 1989. At the very next street, Kleine Rosenthaler Strasse, turn right again (and again, be alert for confusing street signs). The building on the corner (Linienstrasse 206, on your right) is an occupied building, otherwise known as a *squat*. The bright colors of a spider's web and the whimsical prose on the south side of the building are worth a longer look. The verse reads:

Kinder und Narren verlachen das Geld, verachten die Macht, die Menschen ihnen verspricht
Nur Kinder und Narren spielen mit Trümern, sprechen mit Bäumen, wissen dass Mensch das kann
Nur Kinder und Narren leben in Märchen, in Zauberwelten, und glauben daran.

Children and fools mock the money and disdain the
power they are promised
Only children and fools play among ruins, speak to
the trees, and know this can be done
Only children and fools live in fairy tales and magic
worlds—and believe in them.

Poor people's districts rarely have parks and gardens, and
the narrow courtyards between the tenements allowed in
only broken rays of sunlight. Thus, it was on the city's
streets that children played games, traders and merchants
conducted their business, and neighbors chatted after
work. One green exception was the **Garnisonfriedhof**
(Garrison Cemetery) on the left-hand side of Kleine Rosenthaler Strasse. Laid out in 1702 for officers belonging
to the congregation of the garrison, the cemetery was
closed to "newcomers" in 1867 and acquired by the city
in 1900; it was then left alone as a park, "which the
nooks and crannies of this treeless district desperately
need," as a contemporary chronicler observed. Walk inside the wooden doorway and note the fine ironwork on
the crosses. Like Schinkel's exposed red brick, the simple
iron-cast fretwork, for which Berlin metalworkers were
famous, was designed to give Prussian monuments a distinctive style. Not every officer had the means to pay for
a handsome cross, however. After all the money spent
on the showy funeral entourage—which was de rigueur
in society, as Fontane's novels report—the family of Ernst
Ludwig Tippelskirch could not afford iron and had to
make due with tin plates soldered together; the monument is hollow, as a respectful knock will reveal.

To reach **Tippelskirch's grave**, walk about 15 yards
straight and then 15 yards to the left; the dull silver
marker is snug up against a tree. Fine ironwork can be
seen on the three side-by-side markers of the family
Gumtau und von Trützschler, a little beyond Tippelskirch. (Fontane would have loved these names!) Toward
the back, a very fine marker cast like a church steeple is

Garnisonfriedhof

the final resting place of **Daniel Friedrich Gottlob Teichert**. Nearby on the left is the grave of the celebrated **Adolph von Lützow** (1782–1834), one of the leaders of the Freikorps, the volunteer troops that fought against Napoleon in the Wars of Liberation (1813–15). At the entrance, a small exhibition (open every day except Saturday from 10 am to 3 pm) displays helpful historical documents and maps.

As you leave the cemetery, turn left to continue down Kleine Rosenthaler Strasse and take the first left onto Mulackstrasse. Occasionally you may come across street signs that have been blackened over with paint. This technique was used by illegal squatters to confuse West German authorities and speculators who were unfamiliar with the district.

This last leg of the walk—in which we will head along **Mulackstrasse**, across the old Dragonerstrasse (today Max-Beer-Strasse) and Grenadierstrasse (Almstadtstrasse), to Rosa-Luxemburg-Platz—wanders through the heart of the turn-of-the-century Scheunenviertel. As the names Grenadier and Dragoner suggest, the barracks of Prussian soldiers were located along these streets until the middle of the nineteenth century. Beginning in the 1890s, the barracks made way for tumbledown tenements filled with poor immigrants, Jewish and otherwise, who fled poverty in the Ukraine, Poland, and rural Prussia.

Most of these immigrants dreamed of a steamer passage to Manhattan or Hoboken and stopped in Berlin only long enough to change trains, wait for relatives, or save up money to continue their journey. Many immigrants never saved quite enough to continue the voyage but found security and comfort in the growing Jewish community around the New Synagogue. Alexander Granach, later a well-known actor in Jewish folk theaters, felt as if he had never left his native Lemberg in Poland. "I found work," he remembered of his childhood around 1900, "in Grenadierstrasse and felt right at home in this

Berlin. Small, narrow, dark alleyways with fruit and vegetable stands at the corners. Women with painted faces and giant pans in their hands wandered about just like on Stanislau's Zosina-Wolja Lane or Lemberg's Spitalna. Lots of stores, restaurants, shops selling eggs, butter, and milk, and bakeries with the inscription 'kosher.' " Zionists, Hassidic Jews, black coats, and Yiddish theater all made up the Scheunenviertel's vibrant street life and added entirely new elements to Berlin's Jewish community, which until the 1890s had been relatively assimilated into German culture.

Thousands of additional Polish Jews arrived in Berlin during World War I to replace German workers fighting at the front. A final wave of immigration followed the Russian Revolution. War, revolution, and statehood—these events have always created streams of dispossessed people. It is estimated that 40,000 of Berlin's 170,000 Jews in 1925 were Russian and Polish foreigners. Sadly, the same pattern is repeating itself: In the 1990s, ethnic cleansing in Yugoslavia and national chauvinism in Romania have created yet another generation of refugees in and around Berlin.

Jewish immigrants shared the Scheunenviertel and especially Mulackstrasse with all kinds of people: day laborers, hustlers, prostitutes, and gangsters. For every thousand Berliners, there were 1.5 prostitutes in 1925; in the Scheunenviertel, however, the figure was 13.8! The winding streets and interior courtyards of this poor people's district offered excellent cover for illegalities of all sorts. Thousands of tough boys on the run or stateless persons lived in Mulackstrasse or Grenadierstrasse without papers, always eluding the police who maintained order only with great difficulty. One suspected murderer, Rudolph Hennig, evaded police in a daring rooftop escape in February 1906: The young men of the district dressed up in overcoats and hats that matched his, a typical Scheunenviertel comedy that not only mocked the bungling police but greatly complicated their attempts to catch the fugitive. By the 1920s big-city poets and dramatists such as Walter Mehring and Bertolt Brecht transformed neighborhood hustlers into rebellious heroes. "Mack the Knife," the gangster hero of Brecht's *Three-Penny Opera*, would have fit right into this neighborhood.

Like so many other "Berliners," Brecht (1898–1956) was not born in Berlin but adopted the city. Although he lived first on Spichernstrasse (#16) and then, after 1928, on Hardenbergstrasse (#1a), both near the elegant Kurfürstendamm, it was the Scheunenviertel that provided Brecht with his colorful inventory of boxers, bicycle racers, musicians, and gangsters, which he would use again and again in his poetry and plays. Brecht turned against his prosperous Catholic background in Augsburg with a vengeance. He dismissed the pieties with which his generation had gone to war in 1914 and revealed the raw and unsentimental aspects of life. He depicted soldiers as scared, and so he portrayed them with white painted faces. In the same vein, he considered the economic business of modern life nothing more than a criminal spectacle of the strong and clever preying on the foolish.

In Brecht's greatest play, *Three-Penny Opera*, the police work hand in hand with criminals, and beggars work in organized syndicates. Happy endings are for storybooks, Brecht tells his audience, and, accordingly, he complies with a dramatic sleight of hand that saves the hero at the conclusion of the play. For all his Marxism, however, Brecht often confused brutality with cold reason. His mistrust of virtue as mere sentiment led him to make political compromises with the Communist regime after his return to East Berlin in 1948. Nonetheless, Brecht ranks as one of the most important interpreters of modern Berlin, and two important Brecht sites are in the neighborhood. The Theater am Schiffbauerdamm, where *Three-Penny Opera* premiered in 1928 and Brecht and his wife, Helene Weigel, worked in the 1950s, still stands across the Spree from Friedrichstrasse Bahnhof. In addition, Brecht is buried in Dorotheenstadt Friedhof, near the house in which he lived from 1953 to 1956. (At the end of this walk you can reach the cemetery, in which Hegel, Fichte, Arnold Zweig, and Heinrich Mann are also buried, by following Wilhelm-Pieck-Strasse westward, around the Scheunenviertel, to Oranienburger Tor and turn right onto Chausseestrasse [#125]).

The Nazis used the dubious prewar reputation of the Scheunenviertel to tar Berlin's Jews. In the minds of Berliners, the Scheunenviertel was known both as a criminal quarter and a poor Jewish neighborhood. It was thus easy for the Nazis to terrorize law-abiding Jews under the guise of cracking down on illegal activity. The Nazis also tried to associate the older Jewish neighborhood around Grosse Hamburger Strasse with the slums on Mulackstrasse in order to impress upon the minds of Germans the equation: Jews = Criminals.

Today, the Scheunenviertel is fast becoming the fashionable address in Berlin among artists and intellectuals, as the busy efforts at renewal and reconstruction attest. But in the 1920s it was Berlin's most densely populated and impoverished district. Hundreds of residents lived in extreme poverty, holing up in damp cellars or in tiny *entre-sol* apartments. The half-moon window over the entrance at Mulackstrasse 22 denotes an entre-sol, that is, a room between storeys that has ceilings less than 5 feet high. Revised in 1853, Berlin's building codes eventually prohibited entre-sols because they blocked the courtyard entrance to fire engines. Nonetheless, those that remained continued to be rented out to poor families who froze on cold winter floors and never stood upright indoors. Take a look at the old stables in the courtyard of #22, but do so quietly so you don't disturb the neighbors. According to street gossip, #22 was once a Weimar-era house of prostitution. Another entre-sol is located at #31–32, after you cross Gormannstrasse.

On the northwest corner of Mulackstrasse and Gormannstrasse, an empty lot on your left marks the **Mulacken-Ritze**, a famous hangout for pimps and pros-

Entre-sol

titutes and later for uptown slummers such as Bertolt
Brecht. The Mulacken-Ritze, or Mulacken Crack (which a
new same-named cafe farther along this street now honors), still attracted an underworld clientele after World
War II, but it was finally torn down by impatient East
German authorities at the beginning of the 1980s. Mirac-
ulously, the bar's interior has been preserved in the *Grün-
derzeitmuseum*, the only private museum in former East
Germany, in Mahlsdorf (Hultschiner Damm 333; open
Sunday morning), outside Berlin. The museum's founder
is perhaps Germany's most famous transvestite, Charlotte

von Mahlsdorf, who received the distinguished *Bundes-verdienstkreuz* or medal of honor in 1992 in recognition of her tireless efforts on behalf of East Germany's gays and lesbians.

Just ten years ago East German authorities still planned to level all but a few selected streets of the Scheunenviertel. The decrepit buildings and entre-sols that had housed so many impoverished proletarians in the hard luck years of the 1920s and 1930s could not be allowed to stand in the new socialist Germany. As you walk along Mulackstrasse, empty lots indicate the advance of slum clearance. Old tenements were still being dynamited in the spring of 1989 to make way for row upon row of modest concrete apartments with modern amenities. The Revolution of 1989 put an end to this ruthless destruction. In the uncertain legal atmosphere of 1989 and 1990, squatters successfully occupied dozens of buildings slated for demolition, and somewhat later a reunified city administration committed itself to the restoration of the Scheunenviertel. See the beautiful façades at **#11** and, across the street, at **#29–30**, for example. The last house on your right, **Mulackstrasse 37**, was the first building saved by the revolution—but just barely. Four blasting holes in the tile scar the entryway. A last cry of graffiti remembers the dynamite that should have gone into these holes: *Was der Krieg verschonte, überlebte im Sozialismus nicht.* (What the war had spared, socialism did not.)

Mulackstrasse ends at Alte Schönhauser Strasse; we'll be continuing along its extension, Schendelgasse. It's just a short block to Almstadtstrasse, where we will turn left to get to the U-Bahn station on Rosa-Luxemburg-Platz. But first take a look to the right, at the intersection with Hirtenstrasse. An eighteenth-century map of the city in the Märkisches Museum shows a series of long stables around **Hirtenstrasse**, or Shepherd's Street; this is the original location of the seventeenth-century *Scheunen* that gave the quarter its name. Hirtenstrasse was the end of old Berlin; it was a place where cattle and sheep grazed. The sheds are long gone, but the ramshackle slum that was built around them remained. At the beginning of the twentieth century, novelist Joseph Roth described Hirtenstrasse as the saddest street in Berlin. He wrote, "No streetcar runs along it. No omnibus. Rarely even a car."

Turn right at the end of Almstadtstrasse, and you will see the **Volksbühne** on Rosa-Luxemburg-Platz. The theater will be discussed in Walk 3, but it marks the spot of the Scheunenviertel slums that were razed in the first stage (1906) of urban renewal, which has threatened this neighborhood throughout the century. Slip into the subway at Rosa-Luxemburg-Platz or head to Alexanderplatz, down Rosa-Luxemburg-Strasse toward the TV tower.

Rykestrasse Synagogue

Walk · 3

GDGDGDGDGDGDGDGDGDGDGD

Prenzlauer Berg

A PROLETARIAN DISTRICT

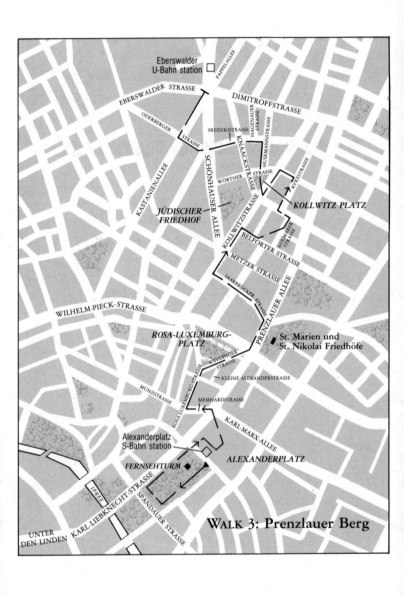

WALK 3: Prenzlauer Berg

Starting Point: Alexanderplatz
Transportation: U- or S-Bahn to Alexanderplatz station
Length: About 2 hours and 30 minutes

Prenzlauer Berg—an area with some of the highest hills in this flat city, hence the somewhat overblown name (*Berg* means mountain in German)—is an old north Berlin working-class district that was largely spared the devastation of World War II. What was once a relatively new neighborhood, built on rolling countryside during the industrial boom at the end of the nineteenth century, now offers a rare glimpse into the long-vanished daily life of ordinary Berliners around 1900. What is more, Prenzlauer Berg remained one of the most interesting neighborhoods during the Communist era. Impoverished streets, disheveled housing, and, behind the façades, an unexpectedly vibrant cultural life gave Prenzlauer Berg an identity all its own. *Kohle und Kunst* (Coal and Art) was the fitting title of one description of the district. And since 1989, "Prenzelberg" has become a new center of the Berlin "scene."

The counterpoint to the neighborhood feel of Prenzlauer Berg is **Alexanderplatz**, a vast square that has been steadily carved out of the tangled medieval core of Berlin. Today, wide right-angled boulevards and immense concrete plazas have obliterated any trace of the narrow streets and tumbledown buildings that once stretched from the palace to the railway tracks. By the end of the nineteenth century Alexanderplatz had already become the hub of municipal traffic and the site of Berlin's central market. Workers in Prenzlauer Berg changed streetcars at Alexanderplatz on their way to work, to register for unemployment compensation, or to browse among the items in the discount department stores. After World War II, Alexanderplatz was redesigned as a showcase for socialist ceremony. With its fountains, discotheques, and restaurants, the "Alex" was where East Berliners met for private and public affairs of all kinds. There is no better monument to the ambitions and pretensions of the old East German regime to recast Berlin in a socialist mold than Alexanderplatz.

Begin on the west side of the Alexanderplatz train station, facing the looming TV tower. There are a few sites of prewar Berlin at the western edge of Alexanderplatz which we will loop down to see, then we will cut back into the thoroughly modern side of Alexanderplatz to see a vast "socialist city" with the enormous **Fernsehturm** as its center. (*Fernseher* is the word for television, but it also means far-seeing, which in the case of this tower is quite appropriate.) Walk down the path to the left of the tower toward the **Rotes Rathaus**, the red-turreted city hall, which stands on the spot of the medieval town hall. This section of the city, one block away from the Spree, was the center of Berlin's early settlement.

This "red" city hall was erected in 1861–69. The handsome brick structure with its distinctive 243-foot-high tower at once recalls the republican municipal edifices of Renaissance Italy and conforms to the spare, cubist proportions that nineteenth-century architect Karl Friedrich Schinkel established for Berlin. Although Berliners have often voted for socialists in the last one hundred years,

Neptune Fountain

the city hall is "red" because of its brickwork, not its politics. If you walk to the end of the plaza and look left, you will see the twin spires of the **Nikolaikirche**, which was built in the early thirteenth century. It has been much altered and reconstructed over time and now has the misfortune to sit in an area gussied up in an unauthentic fashion for the city's 750th anniversary in 1987.

Turn right at the far edge of the plaza and walk past the sumptuous **Neptune Fountain**, designed by Reinhold

Begas in 1891. It once stood a couple of blocks away, on Schlossplatz—on the south side of the palace—and was moved here in 1969. It is worth a closer look and provides a stark contrast to the TV tower and, looking left, the abandoned asbestos-tiled orange-tinted *Palast der Republik* (Walk 1).

Continue across the plaza to the **Marienkirche**, a plain church on a granite foundation that is the second oldest in Berlin, dating from the middle of the thirteenth century. In the intervening centuries it has burned down and been rebuilt several times; its Gothic steeple, for example, was added by Carl Gotthard Langhans, builder of the Brandenburger Tor, in 1788. Inside, the baroque marble pulpit was designed in 1703 by Andreas Schlüter, the same architect who revamped the palace and decorated the Zeughaus, which we saw in Walk 1. Make sure you also see the *Dance of Death*, a mural painting under the tower that mocks the worldly distinctions of refinement, birth, and money which death invariably wipes away. This rare piece of "low culture," the oldest example in Germany, dates from the fifteenth century and was rediscovered during renovations in 1860. The church is open Monday through Thursday, 10 am to 12 pm and 1 pm to 4 pm; Saturday and Sunday, 12 pm to 4 pm.

As you exit the church, walk to the left of the TV tower along Karl-Liebknecht-Strasse toward the elevated S-Bahn train tracks. Nearly a kilometer in length, the present-day Alexanderplatz sprawls over the inner city. This is the result of Allied bombing that devastated the built-up streets between the palace and the S-Bahn station. Originally, Alexanderplatz was a small weekly market just to the left of where the train station sits. A larger square to the right, on the eastern side of the station, also served as a parade ground on which the Prussian king Friedrich Wilhelm II and the visiting Russian tsar Alexander I watched soldiers readying to defeat Napoleon in 1805. To honor the tsar and ally, the old cattle market was renamed Alexanderplatz. As it turned out, the very

next year Napoleon smashed the great European coalition
aligned against him at the battles of Jena and Auerstadt,
occupied Berlin, hauled off the city's treasures, and forced
Prussia to pay a crushing indemnity.

Named in honor of a warlord who was not victorious,
Alexanderplatz remained an undistinguished square until the 1880s when it became an important stop on the
S-Bahn, the municipal railway ring that was completed in
1882. Thirty years later, a total of thirty-four streetcar
lines converged on Alexanderplatz.

In addition, the central food markets were established on the west side of the station in 1886. Like Les
Halles in Paris, Alexanderplatz quickly became a busy
crossroads of crowded streets, streetcars, offices, and
restaurants. To accommodate deliverymen and market
vendors, bars and cafes that were often tucked into the
Stadtbahnbögen (S-Bahn viaduct arches) opened early in
the morning and did not close until late at night. (There
were 731 such arches throughout Berlin, and many still
house handsome shops and restaurants, particularly at
Savignyplatz.) In time, night workers, petty criminals,
and prostitutes also found Alexanderplatz's *Kneipen*
(cafes) and *Budiken* (bars) congenial hangouts. Not surprisingly, the police built their headquarters south of
the square in 1885. Although fashionable department
stores such as Wertheim and Tietz opened their doors
on Alexanderplatz, the square never lost its rough-
edged reputation. Then as now, proper citizens from the
more elegant West End did not often find themselves on
Alexanderplatz.

Alexanderplatz was immortalized in 1929 by Alfred
Döblin, who recreated city sights and sounds in his novel
Berlin Alexanderplatz. He described it in "A Handful of
Men Around the Alex":

> Liquor shops, restaurants, fruit and vegetable stores,
> groceries and delicatessen, moving business, painting
> and decorating, manufacture of ladies' wear, flour and
> mill materials, automobile garage, extinguisher com-

pany: The superiority of the small motor syringe lies in its simple construction, easy service, small weight, small size—German fellow-citizens, never has a people been deceived more ignominiously. . . . Do you remember how Scheidemann promised us peace, liberty, and bread from the window of the Reichstag on November 9, 1918? And how has that promise been kept? Drainage equipment, window-cleaning company, sleep is medicine.

With an eye for revealing detail and an ear for the cacophony of Berliner voices, Alfred Döblin succeeded at something no other writer was able to do before or since: He wrote the "great Berlin novel." Döblin (1878–1957) lived in the city for nearly fifty years before he began *Berlin Alexanderplatz*. For many years he worked as a doctor on the edge of the Scheunenviertel (see Walk 2), a profession that gave him the detached and clinical ability to take apart and reassemble the city. But what made Döblin so successful was his steadfast refusal to try to sum up Berlin. The city remained disorderly and unfathomable, and Döblin left his readers much like his hero Franz Biberkopf: standing alone on street corners, unable to navigate the metropolitan stream.

The loud, confusing, and somewhat disreputable Berlin that Döblin recounted found determined opponents in generations of city planners who endeavored to redo Alexanderplatz in cosmopolitan fashion. Again and again Berlin authorities tried to manage this huge central area. The most recent attempt is in progress right now. But as Döblin foretold, Alexanderplatz has continually eluded architects and designers and will probably never quite fit the conceptions of any master plan.

Now let's pass under the S-Bahn tracks and turn right immediately before the Kaufhaus department store (which housed a Communist-era shopping emporium). At the end of the store building, turn left onto the original site of Alexanderplatz and head toward the right-hand side of the modernist fountain. Long before the East Germans landscaped the region as a socialist parade ground, developers had begun knocking down old buildings and clearing out crooked streets to make way for broader thoroughfares. In the 1920s, Martin Wagner, the city's official planner, reconceived Alexanderplatz as a place to be entirely dismantled and rebuilt every twenty-five years. Improvisation would keep Berlin on the technological cutting edge. The first stages of Wagner's plan were, in fact, realized and are—contrary to design—still standing. Peter Behrens designed the two flanking eight-storey concrete Bauhaus structures (1928–29) on your right in a blatantly functionalist *Neue Sachlichkeit* (New Objectivity) style. In Wagner's vision, the new Berlin had to be functional and adapted to constant change. Old buildings were as useless as broken appliances. As it was, Behrens's structures were not knocked down according to plan in 1954. They survived World War II and the Cold War as office buildings whose strict modernist style is disarmed by kitschy touches such as lace curtains in the windows.

The overwhelming plaza that surrounds you now was redesigned in the 1960s as the centerpiece of the new East Berlin. It truly is one of yesterday's tomorrows. This grand cosmopolitan showcase for the socialist republic is situated at the intersection of huge boulevards that lead south to Unter den Linden and east (ahead of you) to Frankfurter Strasse, the former Stalin-Allee (later named Karl-Marx-Allee) and the traditional parade route along which the Soviet army had advanced into the city in April 1945. Every May Day until 1990, Frankfurter Strasse and Alexanderplatz were festooned with red banners and patriotic slogans.

This very socialist parade ground was also the scene of mass protests against the East German regime. On November 4, 1989, one million ordinary citizens, including many members of the "Party" (the Socialist Unity Party), gathered on the "Alex," holding up a forest of handmade signs that expressed appeals for real change toward democratic socialism. Five days later the Berlin Wall came tumbling down and took with it the hated central committee of old men but also any chance of constructing a better but separate East Germany. The slogan *Wir sind ein Volk* (We Are One People) quickly replaced *Wir sind das Volk* (We Are the People), shifting the emphasis to all-German unity rather than East German reform. As a political symbol and a geographical place, Alexanderplatz has seemed increasingly peripheral ever since that November.

It is astonishing to see how easily socialist architecture has accommodated the signature of capitalism. Signs now advertise Sony, Fiat, and Coca-Cola where placards once hailed the Soviet Union and the collective enterprise. Yet Alexanderplatz is too big for its diminished role in the reunified city. It has become shabby, as if impatiently awaiting the return of grandly choreographed ceremonies and red-flagged parades. Hastily assembled summer beer gardens, flea markets, and weekend concerts simply cannot fill the square or scatter the con artists, hustlers, and other city types more improbable than dangerous who gather here. There was some talk of tearing down the ugly blue-green Forum Hotel and dismantling the television tower in order to redo the square entirely, but that now seems unlikely given the higher-than-expected costs of reunification. As a result, Alexanderplatz will probably remain a vast place that never lives up to the expectations of city planners but, in its obstinate failure to do so, reveals a genuine Berlin liveliness.

Exit Alexanderplatz by walking through the well-marked **Alex Passage** in front of the Forum Hotel, then make a right and enter the underground pedestrian tunnel. Follow signs to Berliner Verlag and Rosa-Luxemburg-Strasse. As you emerge at the corner of Karl-Liebknecht-Strasse and Memhardstrasse, look back down Karl-Marx-Allee at the Lego-like apartment buildings known colloquially as *Arbeiterschliessfächer* (*Schliessfächer* are the storage lockers for luggage you find in train stations; these are storage lockers for workers) that stretch almost as far as the eye can see.

Angle left, then walk a few yards ahead of you on Memhardstrasse to Rosa-Luxemburg-Strasse, and turn right. As you make your way along Rosa-Luxemburg-Strasse toward Rosa-Luxemburg-Platz, you will see remnants of the once modern Bauhaus Berlin of white-collar workers, relentless functionality, and metropolitan traffic that Wagner and his associates attempted to build in the 1920s. Many of these buildings were designed by Hans Poelzig, another premier Bauhaus-style architect. Round corners and the absence of decoration give the buildings on Rosa-Luxemburg-Platz a functional, streamlined look that is characteristic of the Bauhaus school. At the same time, apartments were integrated with stores and theaters and the nearby office buildings on Alexanderplatz, providing a planned neighborhood in a metropolitan center. In each case, Poelzig sought to define style as well as life-style. Today, the once modern apartments at Rosa-Luxemburg-Platz 31–32 are rather neglected. TV antennas drape the front façade, each cord slipping into a different window, giving the whole place an improvised appearance.

The complex at the end of the street, on the right, at Rosa-Luxemburg-Platz 30, was built in 1928–30 and houses **Kino Babylon**. The Babylon is the only surviving movie theater of the golden age of Weimar cinema. It even has the orchestra pit typical of the silent-screen era. Unfortunately, its interior was redone in the 1950s. Nonetheless, the Babylon is now one of Berlin's best repertory theaters and hosts excellent film festivals. For details, check listings in the city entertainment magazines *Tip* and *Zitty*.

Directly ahead of you on Rosa-Luxemburg-Platz is the **Volksbühne**, which looks as though it was built by Poelzig in the 1920s. In fact, the theater was erected by Oskar Kaufmann in 1913–14 in a spare art nouveau style that anticipated the functional sobriety of Bauhaus architects by more than a decade. Like so many other historical buildings in the city center, the Volksbühne suffered during the war when it lost its high gabled roof. Before the war, the stark, sooted façade you see before you was relieved by art nouveau ornamentation.

As its name reveals, the Volksbühne was conceived as a people's theater by the Social Democratic theater club *Freie Volksbühne*, which oversaw its construction. Designed to be a "moral institution," in the words of Germany's great dramatist Friedrich Schiller, the theater not only offered workers inexpensive tickets but produced socially conscious pieces by Henrik Ibsen, Maxim Gorky, and Gerhart Hauptmann. Volksbühne directors included such world-famous figures as Max Reinhardt and Erwin Piscator, both of whom experimented with stage sets and blocking and introduced contemporary themes in classical productions. Friends of the theater attempted to revive the Volksbühne movement after World War II but failed in the face of government opposition. In 1954 the theater was integrated into the Stalinist machinery of official East German culture. Today, however, it is re-emerging as one of Berlin's most innovative and political theaters.

Rosa-Luxemburg-Platz itself is named after Rosa Luxemburg, who along with Karl Liebknecht founded the Communist Party of Germany in January 1919. Although there were plenty of streets and squares renamed by the East German regime to honor party leaders—and an old map will show landmarks bearing the names of forgettable men such as Wilhelm Pieck, Walter Ulbricht, and Otto Grotewohl—Rosa-Luxemburg-Platz stands out. Rosa Luxemburg was a fiercely independent thinker who readily criticized Lenin for his autocratic ways. Unlike Lenin and Trotsky, she condemned all terror, even in the name of revolution. Her example even emboldened free-thinking socialist critics in East Germany who unfurled hand-lettered banners with her words during an

Volksbühne

official commemoration in January 1988: FREEDOM IS AL-WAYS THE FREEDOM TO THINK DIFFERENTLY. The arrest of these dissidents whose only crime was to quote an official hero of the revolution infuriated many East Germans and prepared the dramatic events of 1989. For all these reasons, Rosa-Luxemburg-Platz and the Rosa-Luxemburg U-Bahn station, with its historical collages of her life, are likely to survive the current wave of renaming East Berlin sights.

Loop around the corner of the Babylon and continue on Weydingerstrasse one block to Kleine Alexanderstrasse. This section of Berlin, particularly around Rosa-Luxemburg-Platz, was not only the site of Poelzig's experiments in urban planning but also served as the operational center of the influential Communist Party. The successor party to the East German Communists, the Party of Democratic Socialism, makes its offices in the **Karl-Liebknecht-Haus** at Kleine Alexanderstrasse 18. The Karl-Liebknecht-Haus, named after the socialist orator who declared the stillborn German Socialist Republic from the palace balcony on November 9, 1918 (Walk 1), was also the headquarters of Germany's Communist Party in the 1920s. It charged the neighborhood with the electrical tension of Weimar-era politics. For years, until the Nazi seizure of power in January 1933, huge placards hung on the façade urging Berliners to fight hunger, unemployment, and fascism, and promising a new world of equality and righteousness based on the Soviet Union.

Unfortunately, the Communists fought democrats as well as Nazis. It was in these streets, right outside the Babylon theater, in fact, that Communist gunmen murdered two policemen on the night of August 9, 1931, a crime that remains very much on the minds of Berliners. It turns out that the head of the East German state security forces, Erich Mielke, the mastermind of Cold War spying, was one of the killers. And now, more than sixty years after the event, Mielke has been convicted for this misdeed. It is astonishing how the battles of the Weimar Republic have endured.

When Hitler came to power in 1933, he quickly redressed this neighborhood in fascist garb. From 1933 to 1945 the Karl-Liebknecht-Haus was known as the Horst-

Wessel-Haus (the new name honored a thuggish Nazi streetfighter killed by Communists). Even the Volks-bühne was renamed the Horst-Wessel-Theater.

From the Karl-Liebknecht-Haus it is just two or three turns and a few steps to the foot of Prenzlauer Berg. Leave the Karl-Liebknecht-Haus to your right and continue along Weydingerstrasse to what is still desig-nated Wilhelm-Pieck-Strasse. Make a right and at the busy tram-filled intersection cross Wilhelm-Pieck-Strasse. You are now at the base of Prenzlauer Allee, formerly a trade route leading north from the vanished Prenzlauer Tor. Walk up Prenzlauer Allee one block, cross and turn left into Saarbrücker Strasse, and walk up the steps into the park immediately on your right. Make yourself com-fortable on the benches here, and contemplate the un-believable fact that this used to be the very edge of Berlin. As late as the 1860s, farmers grew grain and potatoes and grazed their cattle on these rolling hills. Eight wind-mills stood in this vicinity as well, on the slopes that provide marvelous views of the city stretching along the Spree Valley.

It is often forgotten that Berlin was more a provincial town than a central capital and remained quite rural until well into the nineteenth century. By 1850, however, Prussia had emerged as a leader in Germany's industrial revolution, and Berlin became a manufacturing hub. Au-gust Borsig established his locomotive factory outside the Oranienburger Tor in 1837, and workers' tenements sprang up throughout the Scheunenviertel, the district below you to the right (see Walk 2). But what historians call Berlin's industrial "takeoff" did not begin until the 1870s when the city became the capital of the unified German Empire. Thereafter, in the space of a single gen-eration, Berlin's population doubled to four million. Thousands of small-town immigrants arrived each week, finding work as maids, waiters, and unskilled workers. Whole new city districts, packed with five-storey tene-ments built around dreary interior courtyards, were hastily laid out in just a few years. One of the most populous districts was Prenzlauer Berg, a working-class neighborhood that stretched up into the hills here. By the 1880s the windmills were just a nostalgic memory, and by the 1920s, Prenzlauer Berg, with 350,000 inhabitants, was the most densely populated urban district in all of Europe. The neighborhood was generally spared during World War II, and very little renovation took place after the war, so the late nineteenth-century aspect of Prenzlauer Berg is still very much evident, although the population has fortunately decreased to 190,000.

Naturally, one million able-bodied workers required dozens of breweries, many of which dotted Prenzlauer Berg. They are all gone now, but three breweries stood on Saarbrücker Strasse alone, including the famous *Bötzow Brewery*, which sat just beyond this grove of trees. Five thousand people could be seated in its sprawling beer garden. A stone monument at the corner of Prenzlauer Allee and Saarbrücker Strasse recalls Bötzow's as one of the organizing sites of the January 1919 uprising led by Karl Liebknecht and Rosa Luxemburg. In March 1919 military airplanes even attacked the brewery in an effort to oust militant Communists. The red-brick buildings of the more tranquil Weissbier brewery are visible across Saarbrücker Strasse on the left.

Walk along Saarbrücker Strasse to get a sense of proletarian Berlin, and don't miss the restored pink **Prunkstück**, the ostentatious "showpiece" at **#15**. Built in 1876, just a few years after unification, this grandiose building anticipates the pompous imperial style that became so popular with the young kaiser Wilhelm II after 1888. Statues of Schinkel and Kaulbach, artists who stood firmly in a classical tradition and would have been horrified at this eclectic ornamentation, peer out from beneath the roof portico. A whimsical verse adds to the parvenu tone of the building:

Jüdischer Friedhof

Einer achts!
Der andere betrachts
Der dritte versachts
Was machts

The first one esteems it,
The other just looks
And the third buys to sell it
What's it matter?

Just beyond #15, take a sharp right onto Kollwitzstrasse. If you wish, stop briefly at the little statue in the square, by the U-Bahn entrance. You will see that it depicts young engravers writing on a mirror-image face. Unveiled in 1892, it commemorates Aloys Senefelder (1771–1834), the inventor of lithography.

As you begin to walk up Kollwitzstrasse, you will see, on your left, across Metzer Strasse on the far side of the empty lot, the windowless brick back wall of a local police precinct that was, until the early 1940s, a Jewish old-age home. To the left of the station lies Berlin's second great **Jewish Cemetery** (Schönhauser Allee 22–23), which is still filled with gravestones. The cemetery is well worth a visit and is open to visitors on weekdays. It has been in existence since 1827 on the city out- skirts; the first cemetery on Grosse Hamburger Strasse (Walk 2) was closed because of the rapid growth of the surrounding neighborhood. But even here, Jews did not rest easily. In the middle of the nineteenth century, King Friedrich Wilhelm III often passed by the ceme- tery on his way to the royal chateau in Niederschön- hausen. Disturbed by the sight of large numbers of Jews attending funeral services dressed in black, he or- dered funeral entourages to use a back gate, the so- called Judengang, for the remainder of his reign (we'll see the gate farther on). Although the cemetery closed in 1880, as the city grew around it, family plots re- mained open until World War II. Giacomo Meyerbeer (1791–1864), the composer; Leopold Ullstein (1826– 1899), publisher of *Berliner Morgenpost*, one of Berlin's biggest and oldest newspapers; and the painter Max Liebermann (1847–1935) are among the famous Berlin figures buried here.

In 1988 hundreds of gravestones here were defaced by neo-Nazis; the police next door allegedly heard and saw nothing. Occurring two years before reunification, the crime revealed the extent to which socialist East Ger- many had its own unresolved problems with the Nazi past and also anticipated the spread of racist incidents throughout Germany in the 1990s.

Continuing a few more steps on Kollwitzstrasse, you can see, on your left, the red-brick walls of the ceme- tery; World War II bombing destroyed the tenements that used to stand on the empty lot. Turn right at Bel- forter Strasse, walk one block, and climb the stairs at the base of the hill across the street on the left. This elevation is the site of one of the main waterworks in the city, erected by the London firm of Fox & Cramp- ton in 1856. Until then, Berliners drew their water from the Spree River and hundreds of privately dug wells.

With thousands of workers crowding into tenement buildings on the city outskirts, a municipal waterworks quickly became a necessity, and the hills of Prenzlauer Berg were high enough to ensure adequate pressure to reach the fifth storey of Berlin's apartments. A huge catchment basin, filled in in the 1950s and now a meadow for sunbathers, received water pumped by huge steam engines at Stralauer Tor, farther eastward on the Spree. The tall, slender tower served as a safety valve in case supply outstripped demand.

As apartment buildings crept farther and farther up Prenzlauer Berg, it was necessary to add another holding tank; the large brick tower at the other end. It was constructed in 1877 and provided pie-sliced apartments for employees of the waterworks; it has now become quite a fashionable address. By the end of the nineteenth century, Berlin residents had running water, although electricity and other amenities did not reach most city people until after World War I. As late as 1927, only 43 percent of Berlin households had electricity, as opposed to 94 percent in Chicago. (To this day, many Prenzlauer Berg apartment dwellers still do not have their own toilets or bathrooms.) Take a moment to enjoy the view of the city spread out below before wandering down the curving path on the other side of the hill.

Coming down from the waterworks, you will find yourself on Kolmarer Strasse; turn left and head up toward the squat water tower. You might want to stop and look at the wonderful new playground on your left. It is full of imaginative mechanical devices such as pumps, mills, pulleys, and chutes, and lots and lots of sand. These marvelously designed and well-maintained playgrounds are a welcome addition to East Berlin, which offered its citizens only a very few, neglected lots. In fact, residents of Prenzlauer Berg used to put together colorful, hand-painted buses that were filled with toys and children's activities and toured the city to offer entertainment to East Berlin's young people.

Kolmarer Strasse, and before that Belforter Strasse and Metzer Strasse—the names of these streets might lead visitors to think they were strolling through the French countryside, but in fact they were laid out just after the Franco-Prussian War of 1870 and commemorate battles won and towns taken. The vaguely worded plaque in front of the large water tower commemorates the victims of Nazism who were tortured in this building, which was used as a concentration camp in the first weeks after the Nazi takeover in 1933. Located in the middle of a working-class district whose residents typically voted for Social Democrats and Communists, the neighborhood prison served to frighten and intimidate political opponents of the Nazis.

At the corner, turn left on Knaackstrasse and then right into Rykestrasse, a typical Prenzlauer Berg street rimmed with late-nineteenth-century tenements. The synagogue of the tiny Jewish community in former East Germany is at Rykestrasse 53. Built in 1903 for a Reform congregation, **Rykestrasse Synagogue** offers a stark contrast with the New Synagogue on Oranienburger Strasse (Walk 2). The synagogue is located behind the front courtyard and does not draw attention to itself. With the rise of anti-Semitism in the 1880s and 1890s, Berlin Jews no longer shared the liberal optimism of their fathers who had built the New Synagogue. As a look through the iron gate reveals, tenement buildings surround the neighborhood synagogue, which probably saved it during the Nazi pogrom on *Kristallnacht* in November 1938 (see Walk 2). Even if neighbors did not think much of Jews, they had no interest in starting a fire that could possibly burn down the block. The synagogue was restored in 1953, after serving the German army as a wartime stable and garage.

Continue along Rykestrasse past the crumbling art nouveau façades at #49–50 and turn left at the end of the block on Wörther Strasse. A few new businesses barely dent the physical dilapidation of these wide proletarian streets. Except for the Volkswagens and Opels that so many East Germans bought once their East marks were exchanged for West marks at a one-to-one rate in July 1990, the streets here have not changed much since the turn of the century. The scarcity of raw materials during World War I and the constricted finances of the Weimar Republic prohibited anything but emergency repairs. You will see many trees dying in this district—a phenomenon that can be traced to leaking gas lines under the sidewalks that have not been replaced or repaired since they were laid, probably in the 1920s. There was also no investment in old housing stock by the East Germans, who preferred to build anew (as we saw in the Scheunenviertel on Walk 2), and many old tenements fell into disrepair. The ubiquitous scars of exposed brick serve as reminders that Berlin is a city of façades; they were often handsomely carved to suggest massive stone foundations, but these are merely trompe l'oeils. Indeed, factories used to offer builders a variety of sandstone façades, a trade that is reviving as the first renovations in a century wrap scaffolding around entire blocks.

In ten years much of Prenzlauer Berg will look polished and clean, a gentrified neighborhood attracting wealthy tenants and upscale shopkeepers who for decades preferred to stay in Berlin's West End, around the Kurfürstendamm. Before that happens, make sure you look at the fading stenciling along the peeling façades, the signature of a working-class neighborhood that had been bustling at the beginning of the twentieth century. Dozens of independent businesses and bars used to line these streets. Many probably never recovered from World War II or were run by proprietors who never came back. Others closed their doors during waves of socialization in the 1950s. The almost vanished advertising painted on the plaster walls recalls a neighborhood of shoppers buying bread or school supplies or wool; of fathers picking up a newspaper or hauling pailsful of coal; of mothers chatting with friends and watching children at play. A coal merchant once had his business at **Rykestrasse 8**;

Melkerei indicates an old dairy at **#7**. At **Wörther Strasse 31** there was even a bookmaker; we can read *Funkbericht von Rennen zu Rennen. Auszahlungen von Rennen* (Races relayed by radio. Payments made here). Next door, at **#30**, *Möbel* denotes a furniture store. Across the street you can make out the offerings of a grocery store: *Eier* (eggs), *Butter, Vollmich* (whole milk), *Obst und Südfrüchte* (fruit and tropical fruits).

The sadness of life in the former East Germany is apparent since these faded signs have no equivalents after World War II. Not only did the raucous life on the streets wither once retailers had closed, but the goods and services they offered disappeared as well. In East Germany it became increasingly difficult to repair shoes, buy hardware, or find quality fruits and vegetables. As a result, an underground barter economy sprang up: piano lessons for plumbing fixtures, kitchen tiles for coal, and so on. After the wall came down, West Germans mocked the greedy purchases of bananas in the East, but they knew little of the privations and the small triumphs that made up daily life in the German Democratic Republic. Because of the absence of a shared history precisely in these small matters, an invisible wall will continue to divide East and West for some time to come.

After one block on Wörther Strasse, turn left onto Kollwitzstrasse. The prospect of gentrification, and particularly the fear of West German speculators arriving in Prenzlauer Berg, has prompted a variety of self-defense measures. Tenants'-rights groups have organized themselves into a dense network as the scattering of leaflets and broadsides in almost any apartment house entryway indicates. Squatters have occupied entire buildings, impeding developers but often making badly needed repairs, while artists anxious for inexpensive studio space are also settling in Prenzlauer Berg. At **Kollwitzstrasse 66**, for example, blue-helmeted surveyors are painted in the entranceway, a cautionary warning to the planners, technocrats, and speculators who are having a field day in reunified Berlin. Even before reunification, this neighborhood had a reputation for unorthodoxy; today, it is rapidly becoming the center of the Berlin "scene." Most of the action occurs spontaneously, in the leafy courtyards behind the tenements where plays and other performances are offered, concerts arranged, and children's parties and barbecues hosted. A few places are accessible to the sightseer, however. Just down Kollwitzstrasse, at #64, is **C. Westphal**, a cafe that is run as a collective. Coffee drinkers and backgammon players give the place a quiet neighborly feeling on a weekend afternoon; the place is packed with convivial drinkers and talkers almost every night. A portrait of Karl Marx overlooks smoky wooden tables and colorful paintings by local artists. Visitors in jeans may feel overly colorful amid the black trousers, black overcoats, black hats, and even black dogs that invariably come with the German alternative scene.

Enter the brightly painted courtyard just past the cafe at **Kollwitzstrasse 64**; a black-and-red flag announces the anarchistic bent of this squat. The **SOS Club** is usually open in the evening and has a "fight the power" sensibility. Women's and lesbian groups meet here on Wednesday; there are live music and videos on Friday; and there is a "trance dance" party on Saturday. House artists have enlivened the gloomy courtyard; one sculpture raises a flag with a 500 mark note from every window, a whimsical play on the red flags that flew from the windows on Frankfurter Strasse every May Day (until 1990) and also an indictment of the new colonial power, the West German mark.

Walk to the end of the block, to the empty lot at the corner. In November 1943 a bomb destroyed this building in which Käthe Kollwitz, the revered Berlin artist, lived in a third-floor corner apartment for more than fifty years. A copy of Kollwitz's statue **Mutterliebe** (Mother's Love) marks the site of her former home; the typically melodramatic East German prose reads:

C. Westphal

"Käthe Kollwitz created this work in the dark days before World War II. The mother wants to save her child, protect it. Where? What from? The darkness threatens fire and murder."

Kollwitz is worth a closer look. She was born into a comfortable family of Königsberg liberals who encouraged her interest in art. Kollwitz's marriage to a young doctor whose Social Democratic convictions led him to work and live among the poor in Prenzlauer Berg solidified her commitment to the politically expressive graphic arts. Both the street and the park across the way are named in her honor.

Kollwitz first came to public attention in the art exhibitions of the Berlin Secession, an influential group of modernist artists and gallery owners at the turn of the century. She gained recognition after almost winning a gold medal at the Greater Berlin Art Exposition held in the Lehrter Bahnhof in 1898. Although Adolph Menzel, the prominent court painter, recommended the award, it was vetoed by Kaiser Wilhelm II who was offended by the subversive nature of Kollwitz's cycle, *A Weaver's Rebellion*, in which downtrodden workers take matters into their own hands. Among her sins, according to the Ministry of Culture, was the depiction of "an assault on an iron gate and the tearing up of the pavement." Kollwitz was never an artist to conform with the establishment. Even among her fellow Secessionists, Kollwitz was defiantly independent in her choice of themes. Although she produced the *Memorial Sheet to Karl Liebknecht*, the murdered Communist, her subjects were mostly individual women and children who in solitude suffered the consequences of the kaiser's war, the Allied food blockade, or the disastrous hyperinflation that followed in 1922–23. Her stark woodcuts bring out the quiet tragedies that Kollwitz saw around her. Instructions to her printers specified dark tones. "Expression is all that is important to me," she wrote, and "the simple line of the lithograph is best suited for that." A trip to the superb **Kollwitz Museum** at Fasenenstrasse 24 in West Berlin also reveals Kollwitz's special attention to the power of the human embrace—arms that hold, protect, caress, reach out, release, and otherwise express the hardships and joys of life. As an older woman, Kollwitz watched Germany's descent into barbarism quietly and sadly. For the second time in a generation, sons and brothers and fathers left for the battlefield (Kollwitz's younger son Peter was killed in World War I; her eldest grandson Peter fell in World War II). After losing her apartment in 1943, Kollwitz moved to a small town outside Dresden where she died a few weeks before the end of World War II.

From Kollwitz's former home, turn and enter the park, **Käthe-Kollwitz-Platz**, across the street. As you do so, look left along Knaackstrasse. A break between the buildings indicates the *Judengang*, the back entrance to the Jewish Cemetery.

In the middle of the park, a sullen, almost forbidding self-portrait of Kollwitz does not seem to keep neighborhood children from frolicking and laughing. Then as now, the park provides tenants with a social center. In the dark days after Germany's defeat in World War I, Kollwitz sat and watched the children play here. Observing their pale, haggard features, she wondered in her diary whether the unwholesome cities shouldn't be abandoned altogether. "Poor children," she wrote in September 1919. "No, there is no other way. The big cities have to be broken up. The only thing that matters is healthy children." Yet two nights later Kollwitz described a very different scene. A full moon had risen over the park, young people were playing mandolins and singing, and the older folks sat on fences and listened. Big cities have always had both their sullen and their unexpectedly happy moments.

Moving to the right of the statue, continue through the park and exit at **Husemannstrasse**. This is a good place to stop and have a drink or a snack at **Bistro 1900**, a modestly priced tavern serving well-conceived continental dishes. Open after noon, the bistro also serves *Rote Grütze*, a wonderful North German dessert made of red currants, berries, and other tart-sweet fruits, and served with cream; it shouldn't be missed. Like the Nicolai Quarter and Sophienstrasse, this one-block stretch of Husemannstrasse was expertly redone to mark the city's 750th anniversary in 1987. Watching craftsmen carefully restore the façades of ordinary tenements, residents hoped that East German authorities would now pay more attention to decaying neighborhoods like Prenzlauer Berg and to the needs of ordinary people. But this was only a showpiece project and did not signal a new political attitude. Some Prenzlauer Berg residents now ironically refer to this street as "Disney World." Nonetheless, Husemannstrasse is a pleasant block with turn-of-the-century lampposts, old-fashioned stenciling, and wrought-iron balconies.

Balconies are to Berlin what gondolas are to Venice, wrote the writers Arno and Karin Reinfrank. No middle-class apartment house was built without them, and in the summer flowers spill from the balconies in a riot of good cheer. In a brilliant sketch about the fast pace of the city, satirist Kurt Tucholsky noted that from time to time he had even seen Berliners sitting out on their beloved balconies: "They must be between phone calls or are waiting for a visitor or, rare as the case may be, they have actually gotten something done early, and so they sit and they wait. But then, from one moment to the next, up they bolt—to the telephone, to the next appointment." The city was always known for its tempo or, as Berliners put it, "tempo, tempo."

Farther up the street there are two wonderful museums. On the right, at Husemannstrasse 8, walk into Europe's only **Friseurmuseum**, or Hairdressing Museum (open every day from 10 am to 4 pm, with extended hours on Tuesday, Wednesday, and Thursday, until 5 pm, and on Saturday until 6 pm), with improbable steam-powered hair-curling irons and a lock of Bismarck's hair on display, among other curiosities. The pride of the museum, which is run by the enthusiastic Jürgen Platow, is the art nouveau interior of the barbershop of François Haby, who became the most famous barber in Berlin because he cut the kaiser's hair. Haby invented the upturned Kaiser Wilhelm mustache and marketed an accompanying mustache wax called Es ist erreicht (Got it). A couple of doors on, at #12, is the **Museum Berliner Arbeiterleben um 1900** (Museum of Working-class Life Around 1900, open Tuesday through Saturday, 10 am to 6 pm, except on Friday when the museum closes at 3 pm). In addition to insightful exhibits on life in former East Germany, the museum displays a typical household of a Berlin worker.

We continue the theme of working-class life as we walk along Husemannstrasse. At the end of the block, take a look at the right angles and broad streets that intersect this sea of tenement buildings. All about you are the signs of nineteenth-century development. The growth of Berlin into a sprawling city of asphalt and stone in the space of a generation made the city the rival of Chicago and Sydney rather than Paris and Vienna, according to contemporary observers such as Walther Rathenau and Mark Twain. The thirty years after unification in 1871 alternated between boom and bust for nimble-fingered speculators. Huge profits could be made developing out-lying countryside into blocks of working-class tenements. New social types joined the cast of Berlin characters: the superrich farmer whose cabbage patch had been sold for millions; the financier who juggled a dozen different deals; and *Trockenmieter*, impoverished tenants who lived in newly constructed buildings only until the plaster walls finished drying, paying in the interim discounted rents and heating the apartments with their winter-cold bodies.

In the face of this explosive growth, it was no surprise that city planners had little chance to lay out new city blocks in the careful, geometric manner of seventeenth-century Friedrichstadt (Walk 1). Metropolitan develop-ment proceeded haphazardly, block by block, so much so that Berlin W (the fashionable West End) was called Berlin WW (or Wild West). In Prenzlauer Berg, however, planners managed the growth of the city with more suc-cess. James Hobrecht, who was Berlin's visionary super-intendent of buildings in the middle of the nineteenth century, insisted on wide residential streets so that in case of fire—always a hazard among so many coal-burning units—the five-storey buildings would topple into the street rather than onto the apartments opposite. Trees prospered on these wide streets as well. Hobrecht also interspersed the new districts with urban parks, such as Kollwitz Platz, though most of the empty lots eventually were overtaken by relentless development. Husemann-strasse was thus a welcome example of city planning even before its 1987 restoration.

Turn left at the corner of Husemannstrasse and Sredzkistrasse. Look down the next street on your right. The right-hand side of Hagenauer Strasse has been nicely restored in the years since reunification, and compared to Husemannstrasse, it gives a much more faithful picture of the mottled sea of stone dwellings that was Berlin in 1900. Farther down Sredzkistrasse, across Knaackstrasse, is another big-city brewery. Built in 1891, **Schultheiss**

Brewery operated here until the end of World War II. It was built by Franz Schwechten, young Wilhelm II's favorite architect, who then moved on to design the Kaiser-Wilhelm-Gedächtnis-Kirche, the ruined church in the heart of West Berlin. Both the brewery and the church reveal Wilhelmine Germany's fancy for decoration. The brewery does not look like a factory but rather resembles a fortress or a temple done up in the popular neo-Romanesque style of the 1890s. Breweries typically delivered their barrels of beer on colorful wagons drawn by *Biergäule*, heavy draft horses. Until the end of the war, horses were tied up at dozens of iron rings that can still be seen around the corner on Knaackstrasse (opposite **#84**). Across from the brewery, a shop at **Sredzkistrasse 6** outfitted teams of horses and their drivers; faint stenciling reveals the words *wasserdichte Pferdedecken*, or waterproof horse blankets.

Declared a historical landmark, the Schultheiss Brewery cannot be altered by the furniture wholesaler who moved in at one end or the *Kulturbrauerei* (culture brewery), an innovative neighborhood cultural center and local television station, at the other end (entrance on Knaackstrasse). At the corner of Sredzkistrasse and Schönhauser Allee is **Franz-Klub**, an alternative music club that existed even before 1989. The Franz-Klub books excellent bands that play everything from the blues to techno-rock, which is postmodern Berlin's original contribution to the music scene.

Now cross the broad Schönhauser Allee and, bearing slightly to the right, proceed down Oderberger Strasse. Oderberger is a tree-lined residential street that has not changed much in one hundred years. Its charms are enhanced by a street festival that local artists organize every year. You can't miss the imposing structure on the left-hand side of the street, which is a **Stadtbad**, or municipal bathhouse, built in 1897. It holds a large swimming pool and also, as the narrow windows indicate, a row of private enclosed bathtubs to which neighborhood people, who lived in tenements without baths, would come once a week to wash. Unfortunately, the pool closed just after reunification; a major overhaul is scheduled to be completed in 1995. In the meantime, the many Prenzlauer Berg residents who live in flats without bathrooms still take their showers here (five thirty-minute showers for 8 marks). Before moving on, have a look at the sculpture above the entrance portal: A shell holds a Berlin bear who is being washed by two nymphs—a service not included in the fee.

At the end of the block, cross over Kastanienallee and again look up and down these ruler-edged streets. At this intersection you can see block after block of apartment buildings. No wonder chroniclers of the city called Berlin a sea of stone. By 1900, Berlin had become a predominantly industrial and proletarian city. Most families had migrated from rural provinces in the south and east, found menial work in the burgeoning metropolis, and established their households in two small rooms, one of which was a sooty kitchen with running water, the other a small family room heated by the coal-burning *Kachelofen*. In 1900 fully 71 percent of Berliners lived in one- or two-room apartments.

Thousands of the tiled ovens are still in use, and other models can be seen at the *Museum Berliner Arbeiterleben*. According to one 1992 estimate, 460,000 Berlin households still heat with the dirty brown coal that is scraped from the earth around Lausitz in East Germany. This means that every winter morning and every winter evening, tenants have to haul buckets of coal from the basement. In older districts such as Prenzlauer Berg, Kachelofen are the rule, although neighborhood coal dealers report the number of customers is steadily diminishing. In a few years the distinctive smell of coal dust in the cold air, which is so evocative of another time, will simply become a nostalgic memory.

Turn right on Kastanienallee and walk into the series of interior courtyards at **Kastanienallee 12**, but do so quietly and circumspectly to respect the privacy of local residents. Three of the four *Höfe*, or courtyards, here survived the war and give an idea of what nineteenth-century tenement life was like. One tenement complex on Ackerstrasse, now vanished, had as many as six courtyards and housed over one thousand people. The dreary uniformity of these dense apartment buildings earned them the name *Mietskasernen*, or rental barracks. Indeed, workers were often treated as conscripts by rapacious employers and greedy landlords and the state that stood behind them.

The two-room flats with which Prenzlauer Berg residents make do today were much more crowded one hundred years ago. Most households included three, four, or more children, as well as a *Schlafbursche*, a tenant who slept in the unused daytime bed or even on top of the family wardrobe. Not surprisingly, Berlin had the highest number of people living in each building at the beginning of the century (76, compared with 38 in Paris and 17 in New York), and Prenzlauer Berg was the most densely populated district in Berlin with 110 people per building. Rooms were all the smaller since housewives often did piecework at home; turn-of-the-century photographs reveal sewing materials heaped on beds, kitchen tables, and counters. Poorer families lived in the wings built along back courtyards—which were entirely cut off from the light of day and the noise of the street—or in damp subterranean rooms.

Most tenants lived impoverished lives around the interior courtyards far from the street. Although courtyards quickly became the center of apartment life, they were usually only big enough to meet municipal codes. After the Revolution of 1848 and dangerous outbreaks of cholera, the Prussian state finally set building standards and fire codes (1853). Fire engines and their high-perched coachmen had to be able to enter all courtyards; the front entrance therefore could not be blocked by a low-hanging entre-sol apartment (see Walk 2). Moreover, courtyards had to be at least 17 feet by 17 feet, the turning radius of the engines. Hand-pumped water reached no higher than 68 feet, which set the maximum height for apartments, limiting them to about five storeys. In his novel of Berlin in the hard-luck 1930s, *Mr. Norris Changes Trains*, Christopher Isherwood described these spaces in the stone sea: "The courtyard was narrow and deep, like a coffin standing on end. The head of the coffin rested on the earth, for the house fronts inclined slightly inward. . . . Down there, at the bottom . . . the rays of the sun could never penetrate."

As late as the 1930s, tenants still raised goats, chickens, and even oxen in the interior courtyards while factories and workshops occupied the ground floor of many of these mix-used buildings. These dirty, busy places were also the only place for neighborhood children to play. Occasionally an organ grinder, wandering from one courtyard complex to another, came around. This was a joyous moment in the *Hof*; children would dance and run up to their parents to ask for a 5-pfennig piece to tip the musician. Children also put on plays and dress balls, mimicking the finer arts downtown. The courtyards also revealed the grim poverty of residents, however; neighbors overheard the sounds of family fights, and disease, alcoholism, and prostitution were prevalent as well.

After World War II, municipal authorities in both East and West Berlin began to tear down the backyard buildings in order to alleviate overcrowding and to create parks and parking places behind the street-front buildings. As a result, vintage prewar courtyards like the three here at Kastanienallee have become increasingly rare. Given the low supply of housing in present-day Berlin, however, the remaining *Seitenflügel* and *Hinterhäuser* (side wings and back buildings) will stay standing for some time. Many city residents cherish these closed-off interior spaces. Although they still have to put their heads all the way out the window to find out the weather outside, tenants also enjoy tranquility in the middle of the busy city that is difficult to imagine. Residents in the Kastanienallee have also fashioned an infectious neighborhood sociability. Walk through to the small park at the end of the courtyards. Hand-wrought sculptures, playgrounds, and even a small outdoor theater give the complex a wonderful vitality. The garden area extends farther than is immediately apparent: Follow the path around to the right and keep going until you get to the small amphitheater at the end. The old ornamental stone fragments and even a Prussian eagle scattered about supposedly were retrieved by well-connected tenants from the ruins of the kaiser's palace after it was blasted in 1951. The story is too good not to be true.

Retrace your steps to exit this apartment complex, then turn left on Kastanienallee and head to Kastanienallee 7–9. This is the well-marked location of the **Prater**, an old-fashioned beer garden. Before tenement buildings filled Prenzlauer Berg, the Prater was the destination of Sunday excursions into the countryside. Huge trees shaded a comfortable beer garden that the Pfeffer Brewery opened prior to 1844. Over the decades the city gradually encircled the Prater. By the 1870s the Prater gardens could seat four thousand; the mostly working-class patrons came to drink beer, enjoy variety shows, and dance. As an increasingly metropolitan place of amusement, the Prater added a movie theater in 1916. Frida Leider, a young working-class girl, remembered a trip to the Prater as the high point of her childhood summers before World War I: "Of course the children had to get there by noon in order to reserve the best places at the cheap tables, even though the show didn't start until four. We defended these places like lions. . . . Thank God, around two, our mother arrived with all sorts of cakes and cookies. I couldn't sit still waiting for the curtain to rise." Dancing followed in the evening. Thereafter, "we got our grilled sausages to eat, and finally at ten sharp we were all dragged kicking and screaming home to bed." Unfortunately, the Prater beer garden closed in 1990, but it is scheduled to reopen after renovations have been completed. Let's hope so because the Prater is a Berlin original from a preindustrial time.

Across from the Prater, check out **Das alte Photo**, an antiquarian bookshop that also sells old postcards, and **Galerie am Prater**.

At the end of Kastanienallee is one of Berlin's busiest intersections and one of its most metropolitan corners. Kastanienallee, Pappelallee, Eberswalder Strasse, Dimitroffstrasse, and Schönhauser Allee all come together amid the steel structures of the U-Bahn line, various streetcar tracks, bus routes, and the passage of hundreds of cars and pedestrians; only horse-drawn wagons are missing. This is what cities looked like before superhighways sliced them up and suburban life-styles emptied them out. The distinctive features that enhance this urban landscape have been here for almost a century. On the corner stands the **Litfasssäule**, or advertising pillar. These pillars were designed by Ernst Litfass as a way to clean up the disheveled look of notices and advertisements pasted haphazardly on trees, sandstone façades, and wooden fences. The first 150 pillars (each 9.5 feet high and 9.75 feet in circumference) were placed on Berlin street corners on July 1, 1855, an event honored by the *Broadside Polka*, composed by the well-known musician Kéler Béla. By the onset of World War I there were almost two thousand Litfasssäulen in Berlin and thousands more around metropolitan Europe. However, the order that the pillars were supposed to impose on the city gave way to new kinds of disharmonies as art *nouveau* artists designed posters with bold typography and bright colors which collided in an exuberant big-city collage. To this day Berliners rely on Litfasssäulen to find theater and film listings as well as notices for upcoming political events.

If the Litfasssäule belonged to strollers along the boulevard, the newspaper kiosk belonged to streetcar and subway commuters who bought a daily paper on their way to and from work. The first kiosks were opened along with the Stadtbahn ring in 1882. Others followed the extension of the U-Bahn lines, which reached into Prenzlauer Berg in 1911. When the Prussian police relaxed laws against curbside shopping in 1904, entrepreneurs quickly sought licenses to open kiosks on busy corners as well. During the 1920s—the golden age of the Berlin press—kiosks sold the ninety-three different newspapers that appeared each and every week in Berlin, as well as out-of-town papers and hundreds of magazines. A few old-fashioned eight-sided kiosks are still open in Berlin, and smaller ones abound in U-Bahn and S-Bahn stations (as they do here), but they no longer introduce city people to city life the way they once did. Too many Berliners now move through the city privately, in their own cars. While streets are much more crowded with automobile traffic, the sidewalks and streetcars are much emptier today than they were fifty or eighty years ago.

Of course, people still go outside, and on a cold winter's day (or in any other season, for that matter) there is nothing better than a *Thüringer* or a *Weisswurst* or a *Currywurst* with *Pommes frites*, a cold beer, or perhaps a glass of hot *Glühwein* (mulled wine) at one of Berlin's thousands of *Buden*, or snack bars. Many are even open on Sunday. One of the most famous of these is **Konnopkes Würstchenbude**, practically in front of you under the U-Bahn tracks at Dimitroff and Schönhauser Allee. It has been serving Prenzlauer Berg since 1930 and is known especially for its delicious Currywurst. When one of Konnopke's employees takes your order, what you want to say is: "*Eine Currywurst, bitte. Pommes frites und dazu ein Bier.*" (A Currywurst, please. French fries and also a beer.)

To get back to the city center, take the elevated U-Bahn to Alexanderplatz.

Walk · 4

▰▰▰▰▰▰▰▰▰▰▰▰▰▰▰▰▰▰▰▰▰

Kreuzberg

EXPERIMENTS IN DIVERSITY

Kreuzberg Façade

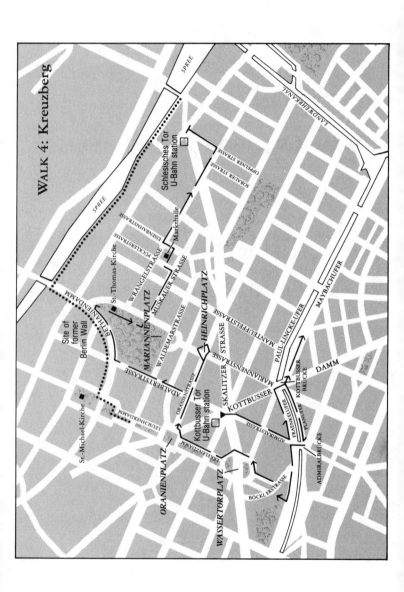

WALK 4: Kreuzberg

Starting Point: Kottbusser Tor
Transportation: U-Bahn to Kottbusser Tor station
Length: About 3 hours

The best time to see the Turkish market is Tuesday or Friday afternoon; otherwise, afternoons offer the best neighborhood views.

Before reunification in 1989, Berlin enjoyed a dubious reputation among West Germany's solid taxpayers. After all, Berlin was accessible only by crossing the dangerous "red sea" of Communism. Parents even refused to send their children on school-sponsored bus trips to the former capital since for three or four hours, children from the "West" would be "captive" on transit routes through the "East." Moreover, the beleaguered former capital had strange customs of its own. Berliners had always been known for their *Schnauze*, or their lip, their impertinence. They were also politically suspect; it was to West Berlin, for example, that German draft dodgers fled to escape military service, which did not apply to residents in a city officially occupied by the Allies—the case until 1990. As a result, Berlin's universities overflowed with students and permanent students, who established a lively alternative left-wing "scene" of hippies, Maoists, "Greens," and punks. Tabloid newspapers depicted Berlin as a city largely abandoned by taxpayers and merchants and left to these new-age "barbarians." Berlin also had the largest number of foreigners of any German city. Turkish immigrants, especially, gave Berlin a distinctive international flavor.

What was true of Berlin was doubly so of Kreuzberg. This district in West Berlin made headlines throughout the 1970s and 1980s as the site of various experiments in alternative living; as the stronghold of the leftist terrorist group, the Red Army Faction; and as the home of some 40,000 of Berlin's 135,000 Turks. For all the talk of the "People's Republic of Kreuzberg," however, the deutsche mark remains the medium of exchange, a direct bus (#129) runs to and from the very bourgeois Kurfürstendamm, and punkish anarchists push their well-dressed kids around in high-tech strollers and even greet one another at protest marches by politely shaking hands. Residents refer to Kreuzberg as the *Kiez*—loosely meaning the "scene" or "hood"—an extended family of a neighborhood that is a bit rebellious but also charming and eclectic, a refreshing counterpoint both to the "Ku'damm" and to Alexanderplatz. Kreuzberg comes alive in the late afternoon, which is the best time to take this walk.

The best way to enter Kreuzberg is to arrive by subway (lines 1, 12, and 15) at Kottbusser Tor. Walk down the stairs at the far west end of the station (following signs to Wassertorplatz), turn right, and cross Skalitzer Strasse. Walk a few yards to the right to the bustling intersection around **Kottbusser Tor**.

Like Prenzlauer Berg, Kreuzberg was laid out during the building boom that followed German unification in 1871. In the space of a few years, streets were carved out of muddy potato fields, and tenements were raised along sheep meadows. With an excellent network of canals and nearby railways, Kreuzberg quickly attracted factories and workshops, which colonized the interior courtyards and ground floors of tenement buildings. These mixed-use buildings became typical of the neighborhood. The district was home to both the middle classes and workers whose livelihoods revolved around the many thriving businesses located here. Kreuzberg was badly battered during the Allied bombing raids, however, and its industrial base never really recovered. Perhaps the most famous photograph of Berlin in 1945 shows a desolate moonscape of gutted buildings and freestanding façades along Kreuzberg's Dresdener and Alte Jacobs Strasse. Postwar city planners consequently targeted Kreuzberg for extensive redevelopment, but their solutions—graceless, impersonal towers of concrete—only left the neighborhood looking more desolate. Urban renewal eventually sparked fierce battles between tenants and technocrats that indelibly shaped Kreuzberg's present-day identity.

The construction of the Berlin Wall in 1961 compounded Kreuzberg's troubles. The wall enclosed the neighborhood on two sides, and the Landwehrkanal formed a boundary on a third. Businesses, many of which lost skilled workers because they were stranded in East Berlin, relocated to more centrally situated neighborhoods in West Berlin or left the isolated city altogether. For more than two decades Berlin's economy shriveled and was only resuscitated by the millions of marks that came every year from Bonn. Given the sky-high rents in Berlin today, it is hard to imagine that Kreuzberg was known as an affordable neighborhood, ideal for impoverished students and draft dodgers, for "guest" workers from Turkey who arrived to make up the city's labor shortage, and for starving artists who converted the district's abandoned factories into studios. In less than a generation the Cold War had completely transformed the character of the neighborhood. A visit to Kreuzberg is thus another installment in Berlin's story of constant change.

At Kottbusser Tor you will likely feel as if you have

been transported to a Third World metropolis of poured concrete buildings, ceaseless traffic, and loud political sloganeering. The large complex that dominates the square is the **Neues Kreuzberger Zentrum** (NKZ), a government-funded housing project. Completed in 1974, the NKZ represented the first stage in an ambitious modernization plan that envisioned a city of satellite neighborhoods connected by superhighways—Berlin's partner city is Los Angeles, after all. That the NKZ was not designed as luxury housing is evident: Apartments were simply stacked on top of each other. Function and economy overruled aesthetics and resulted in anonymous and alienating structures. Apparently the iron girders of the NKZ are rusting so that extensive renovations will be necessary soon; some Kreuzbergers hope the complex will be torn down entirely.

As you look around the NKZ complex, you will notice the swirls of graffiti with which all sorts of left-wing groups have adorned Kottbusser Tor. The countless variations of German Marxists have now made room to accommodate Turkish and Kurdish counterparts. Along walls you will often see "TKP/ML (B)," for example, a ponderous acronym that stands for a particular Marxist-Leninist line of a Kurdish Communist party. Other graffiti condemns the 1991 Gulf War or supports the Maoist Shining Path guerrillas in Peru. One banner on the wing of the NKZ that straddles Adalbertstrasse celebrates the (purely imaginary) "revolutionary partnership" between Kreuzberg and Ayacucho, the Andean city that spawned the Shining Path. Most of the German Left does not take these fringe groups seriously, although they tag along in neighborhood *demos* (demonstrations).

The construction of the NKZ generated a broad-based tenants'-rights movement that united long-haired activists and middle-class shopkeepers. Local residents resented the thoughtless design of the housing project and the ill-considered destruction of disheveled but still sturdy prewar buildings. After a decade, the generally peaceful

Neues Kreuzberger Zentrum

protests culminated in illegal occupations of more than one hundred condemned buildings and genuine street battles at Kottbusser Tor in 1979 and 1980. Since then, Kreuzbergers have upheld their insurrectionary tradition—too punctiliously, perhaps. Anti-American riots broke out when President Ronald Reagan visited Berlin in June 1987, for example. And every May Day and October 3, the Day of German Unity, the radical Kreuzberg scene shows its antiestablishment colors amid columns of riot police.

Retrace your steps from the NKZ complex to the intersection of Skalitzer Strasse and Admiralstrasse. Cross under the train tracks to the other side of Skalitzer Strasse. Here, too, you see the large and impersonal apartment buildings favored by city bureaucrats. But Kreuzberg's Turkish flavor is immediately apparent as well. Many of the families in Kreuzberg are Turkish and do their banking and shopping in the dozens of Turkish grocery stores, bakeries, and delicatessens throughout this neighborhood. For more than ten years, from 1961 to 1973, the German government staffed recruiting offices throughout Turkey, inviting workers to fill the thousands of menial and manufacturing jobs that Germans were no longer willing to do themselves. A large number of immigrants went to Berlin where the labor shortage was particularly severe. About 300 Turks, mostly students, were living in Berlin when the wall went up. Eight years later, there were 70,000. In the 1970s, when more and more Turkish workers decided to make their home in Germany and sent for their families, the number reached 170,000. At one point Berlin was the fourth-largest Turkish city in the world, after Istanbul, Ankara, and Izmir. As a result of the fast pace of urbanization in Turkey, however, Berlin has now dropped to twentieth place.

Although Germany does not naturalize or offer citizenship to immigrants, a subject of much debate, the Turkish community is a permanent part of German life. In fact, Berlin has had a cemetery for Moslems since 1798, the so-called Turkish Cemetery near Tempelhof Airport (Columbiadamm 128), which King Friedrich Wilhelm III purchased to provide a final resting place for the first Ottoman ambassador to Prussia, Ali Aziz Efendi, who died while serving his empire in Berlin. Today, Turkish children grow up here and go to German schools, and most immigrants (83 percent) have no intention of returning to Turkey, which for them has become a foreign place.

Walking down Admiralstrasse, away from the train tracks, you will see that the tenants' movement should be credited with creating a more livable neighborhood. After 1974, plans for large complexes like NKZ were abandoned in favor of smaller and more aesthetically pleasing housing projects.

The **hourglass statue** by Ludmilla Seefried-Matejkova in the intersection of Admiralstrasse and Kolfurter Strasse is a whimsical perspective on the history of the world according to the Kiez. An authoritarian and "bourgeois" past is symbolized by a pair of bronze admirals, representatives of the Prussian civil servants who used to live in Kreuzberg. They have nothing in common with the rebellious punker and unemployed youth, who are rendered as sympathetic but rather solitary figures. If the past is depicted too one-dimensionally as a faraway, strait-laced sort of place, the present seems a bit lonely and unforgiving; there is a somber undertone to this playful piece.

Cross through the intersection and continue on the walkway (which is still Admiralstrasse) between the flanking wings of a handsome red-brick grammar school. This school is an example of an essential neighborhood institution that city technocrats amazingly had neglected to plan for when they built the NKZ, and which they added only as a result of public pressure.

Move on now to where the street begins again. At this point you'll see a **wall mural** on the left and a **brick wall sculpture** to the right. City planners originally called for *Flächensanierung*, a carpet-bombing approach to urban renewal, that met with the tenacious resistance of residents. According to one estimate, 70 percent of the destruction Berlin suffered between 1942 and 1952 occurred *after* 1945 at the hands of city planners; and much more took place between 1952 and the late 1970s moment when ambitious technocratic blueprints suddenly lost their allure. In any case, the razing crews in Kreuzberg were finally stopped by citizens just past the school at Admiralstrasse 23. The scars that bulldozers scraped on the side of this prewar building have been cleaned up, replaced now by the mural that you see ahead of you, entitled *Kein Abriss*, or Don't Tear It Down.

The mural does not sentimentalize the neighborhood it honors. It depicts an old pensioner watching television, an alcoholic sitting at the kitchen table, and on the street side, a small shop typical of the enterprises ignored by city planners. The punker scrawling the title of this piece on the wall and the baton-waving policeman threatening the young man recall the decisive street battles of the 1980s.

The cartoonlike figure with the baton was the part of

the mural that caused a huge public outcry. While Kreuzberger residents may have found the menacing cop fa-
miliar, conservative politicians did not. Police were
disciplined law enforcers rather than aggressive lawbreak-
ers, they argued, and demanded the artist retouch the
mural. The issue actually bounced around in the courts
for some time. Eventually, someone leaned a ladder to
the side of the building, measured the baton, measured
also the distance between the tip of the baton and the
head of the punker, and established that the cop could
not have hit the kid and consequently could not be regarded as brutal, and therefore the honor of Berlin's finest
was left intact. The mural stayed.

Across the street, at Admiralstrasse 15, a handsome
brick sculpture, *Neues Leben in Alten Steinen*, or New Life
in Old Stones, expresses the rallying cry of the tenants'
movement. Although the remaining stretch of old-brick
tenements on Admiralstrasse was saved, this particular
sculpture had to be dismantled shortly after it was completed and rebuilt with brand-new bricks; apparently a
sharp-eyed Prussian bureaucrat discovered a law that
prohibited the reuse of old bricks!

You want to continue walking on the left-hand side
of Admiralstrasse so you can see the buildings at Admiralstrasse 15, 16, and 17, which display a variety of postwar renovations. **Number 15** was restored as a period
piece for the 750th anniversary of the city in 1987. **Number 16**, an old building, has been completely refitted as
a modern cooperative in which residents determine the
layout of their apartments. From the street you can see
that each balcony is used somewhat differently. The least
expensive renovation, at **#17**, is also the least pleasing.
Throughout the 1950s and 1960s, workers would erect
scaffolding, knock off the prewar sandstone façade, and
slap on all-weather plastering; these basic facelifts took
three or four days and can be seen all over Berlin.

At the end of this block, cross over Fraenkelufer, and
before the bridge turn left to walk along the tree-lined

banks of the **Landwehrkanal**. Landwehrkanal—the first association that comes to mind for most Berliners is the gruesome 1919 deaths of Karl Liebknecht and Rosa Luxemburg, whose body was dumped in the Landwehrkanal. Their murder by reactionary mercenary veterans of World War I not only anticipated the violence of the Nazis but also deeply divided Social Democrats and Communists and kept the two working-class parties from working together to fight Nazi brownshirts in the 1930s. Their murders resonate through the unhappy history of twentieth-century Germany. Both were prominent Social Democrats who deplored their party's patriotic stance during World War I. During the November 1918 Revolution, they formed a small splinter group that opposed the moderate course of the mainstream Social Democrats. In early January 1919, the Spartakus League (the kernel of the Communist Party) tried to jump-start the stalled revolution by occupying government buildings on Wilhelmstrasse. Although few Berliners supported the Spartakists, fewer still endorsed the right-wing mercenaries whom the Social Democratic government deployed to crush the uprising. Liebknecht and, especially, Luxemburg, a fiercely original thinker who always commanded the respect of her party opponents, were regarded by the rank and file more as wayward siblings than as political enemies.

After several days in hiding, Luxemburg and Liebknecht were arrested on January 15 and taken for interrogation to the Eden Hotel in the Tiergarten, which served as army headquarters, and then driven to Moabit Prison. It quickly became apparent, however, that their captors had no intention of delivering them to the prison. Even as Liebknecht and Luxemburg left the Eden, officers in the lobby demanded their immediate execution, and an infantryman smashed Luxemburg with his rifle butt. Several minutes later, Liebknecht's convoy stopped abruptly in the middle of the park; the driver claimed a flat tire. Liebknecht was ordered out and simply shot. Packed into another car, Luxemburg was killed by an unknown assailant who jumped on the running board and then fled into the night. Instead of being delivered to the morgue, her body was unceremoniously thrown into the Landwehrkanal from the Lichtenstein Bridge in the Tiergarten. The badly decomposed body of Rosa Luxemburg was not found until many months later. A monument in the Tiergarten commemorates the murder that haunted the city and divided its people.

"Es schwimmt eine Leiche im Landwehrkanal" (A corpse is swimming in the Landwehrkanal), a popular revue song of the 1920s, stared the everyday violence of Weimar Germany straight in the face. Not only Luxemburg but the bodies of Berlin's murdered children and lonely suicides were frequently fished out of the canal. Käthe Kollwitz, Heinrich Zille, and other artists all depicted the last sad steps of a penniless mother and child toward the dark canal. A walk along the Landwehrkanal, which reflects the jagged profile of old and new in its melancholy waters, brings to mind these and other tragedies of Berlin's history.

The Landwehrkanal was originally excavated in 1845–50. Six and one-half miles long, it connects the Upper Spree at Schlesisches Tor with the Lower Spree in Charlottenburg, and by opening the western and southern precincts of the city to river traffic, it contributed greatly to the economic development of Berlin. In the age before railways, waterways were the most economic way to ship materials. Thanks to the canal, coal, peat, gravel, lumber, and bricks, which otherwise had to be drawn by horses, could be transported easily to building sites. Traffic was so dense that the canal had to be widened in 1883–89, although today only a few pleasure crafts and sightseeing boats make use of it. The banks of the Landwehrkanal, on the other hand, are favorite paths for morning, afternoon, and evening walks. Along with the elevated tracks of the S-Bahn and the U-Bahn, the Landwehrkanal breaks up the city's uniform and stony face and offers the sightseer views with some perspective and

depth. Quiet stands of trees, the stately façades of turn-
of-the-century apartment buildings, swans and ducks, and
the soft glow of hundreds of gas lanterns make the Landwehrkanal Kreuzberg's most elegant thoroughfare. "I
know another Berlin," wrote Erich Weinert, a hometown
poet, in 1927:

> Where chestnuts bloom along the Landwehrkanal,
> Where sailors will sing their hometown songs,
> And the noise of the street does not drift over,
> Where geraniums bloom in front of small windows,
> There Berlin is different and still and dreamy.*

About midpoint on this one-block stretch of the canal, at
Fraenkelufer 10–16, is what remains of the Orthodox
Lindensynagoge, once one of Berlin's three largest tem-
ples. Built in 1913–16, it was badly damaged during the
November pogrom in 1938, although a Jewish kindergarten remained open until January 1942. Allied bombers
destroyed the building in 1945. The ruins of the main
synagogue were torn down in 1958, so all that remains
today is a side building.

Turn right at the end of this block and cross Kottbusser Brücke. On the other side of the bridge you have
a choice of turning right and returning to Admiralstrasse
along Planufer on the opposite bank of the Landwehrkanal, or turning left and crossing Kottbusser Strasse to
Maybacher Ufer to see the **Turkish market** that takes place
every Tuesday and Friday. If you're going to explore the
market, read on; otherwise, skip ahead to page 175. But
before continuing the walk, consider whether you want
to stop for light refreshments in one of the four cafes
(**Exil**, **Uebersee**, **Jones**, and **Klassik**) back on the other
side of the bridge. In the summer, the outdoor tables at

---

*Erich Weinert, "Ich kenne ein andres Berlin,"
cited in Hermann Kahler. *Berlin—Asphalt und Licht*
(Verlag das europaische Buch: Berlin, 1986), 150.

Turkish market

these cafes on Paul-Lincke-Ufer are popular gathering spots for strolling Berliners, Kreuzberg residents, and tourists. On the Maybacher Ufer, you can also sit at the canal's edge to watch swans and sightseeing boats ply the waters at the **Ankerklause**, by the bridge. A couple more outdoor cafes can be found along Planufer (**Kaefer-kopf** at 92d and **Falscher Hase** at 92c) and farther along is an Irish pub (**The Barge**), also with outdoor seating. This outdoor cafe life is one of the reasons the Landwehr-kanal is so popular.

On Tuesday and Friday a one-block stretch of Maybacher Ufer is closed to cars to make room for the delightful Turkish market. German food has its whole-some virtues, but variety typically is not one of them. Thank goodness for Kreuzberg and the Turkish market where you can pick up sharp spices and chili paste, a dozen varieties of olives, hunks of sheep's and goat's cheese, prepared salads, and rounds of delicious Turkish bread (*Fladenbrot*). While at the market, don't forget to get yourself a *döner kebab* (a grilled lamb sandwich in Turkish bread, topped with tomatoes, lettuce and/or cabbage, and a deliciously garlicky sauce), the best this side of Istanbul's spice market; the **Lale Imbiss** at Maybacher Ufer 8 offers an excellent and spicy döner, for example. Or if you are more in the mood for a sit-down meal, **Bolu Grill Evi** (at the corner of Maybacher Ufer and Kottbusser Strasse) offers a tempting array of traditional Turkish dishes. The windows in front display sides of grilled lamb and pork.

At least half of Berlin had not tasted a döner kebab when the wall came down in November 1989, and it was not immediately clear how East Berliners would react to the international tastes of places like Kreuzberg. Most *Ossies* (the West's name for *Ost* or East Germans) went first to the Kurfürstendamm to spend the one hundred marks that every visiting East German received as "welcome money" from the West German government. At least one young Berliner found, however, that he loved döner kebabs. He tried to save his Western marks to buy something more substantial, but with each trip to West Berlin he ended up buying a mouth-watering döner. When the hundred marks was gone, he started changing his East German marks at terribly unfavorable rates to feed his craving for döner kebabs. Now, döner kebab stands can be found throughout the unified city, and this Turkish specialty has become as typical of Berlin cuisine as a Currywurst or a Spreewald pickle.

After a tour of the one-block market, return to Kottbusser Brücke and continue down the other side of the Landwehrkanal on **Planufer**. This block is lined with beautiful turn-of-the-century residential apartments that are the result of another of the housing battles that seem to be endemic to Kreuzberg's history. It was in the summer of 1872, along this side of the Landwehrkanal, that poor immigrants who had arrived in the booming city to make their fortunes but had been unable to find affordable housing cobbled together *Freistadt Barackia*. A contemporary newspaper described this poor people's city in pitiful detail: "Hastily built plankboard shacks have been built in the open, right in the middle of potato fields and meadows. Rain leaks through the roof, and the wind blows through the finger-wide cracks in the walls. On one side is a wooden door; on the other, a few small windows. A piece of stovepipe is stuck between the planks on the third side." It wasn't long before the Prussian police moved in to dismantle the sheds and barracks, disperse the crowds, and secure the grounds for the construction of the affluent apartments that you see before you. For the homeless workers, there was little available except for tenement cellars or an itinerant fate as *Trockenmieter*, the impoverished tenants who lived in otherwise unaffordable new apartments for the six to twelve months that it took the plaster walls to dry.

At the end of this block, cross the Landwehrkanal over the Admiralbrücke and turn left on Fraenkelufer. The peach and apricot colors of the housing project at the corner and, farther on, at **Fraenkelufer 38**, are a refreshing counterpoint to the Neues Kreuzberger Zentrum at Kottbusser Tor. Walk on to **#38**. Built in the mid-1980s, only some ten years after the NKZ, this complex was designed by Berlin architects Inken and Hinrich Baller in cooperation with local neighbors and future tenants. Whimsical angles and curves and colorful pastels add a touch of Miami Beach to the gray North German cityscape. Although critics mocked the postmodern apartments as a frivolous mix of "Black Forest sanatorium and hotel paradise," they are very popular with residents. Walk through the pillared entry at #38 into the expansive courtyard, which comprises a full city block that has been "cored"—the apartments that used to cluster around the interior have all been torn down. The resulting space is attractively landscaped and provides residents with a cherished bit of "country" in the middle of the city. All in all, the Baller complex is much more successful and, in fact, was no more expensive to build than the NKZ.

Bear left through the interior courtyard, cross the

footbridge, and walk down the gravel path to exit through a second entrance (at #44), which returns you to Fraenkelufer. Cross the street to the canal, bearing right, and follow the shallow circular steps down to the water's edge. The canal was once twice as wide at this point and formed an urban harbor; barges bearing fruits and vegetables would come from as far as the Spreewald, sixty miles to the south, to unload their produce, which was then delivered to markets and stores around the city. A feeder canal from the Spree, the **Luisenstädtischer Kanal**, joined the Landwehrkanal at this point as well. In fact, Berlin used to boast of having the second-largest inland harbor in Europe. All this busy shipping activity is long gone; the harbor was filled in in the 1960s and became a park.

You might want to relax on the grass here under the willows or sit on one of the whimsically designed benches scattered along this greenway. You can walk through this pleasant park by taking the first stone-lined gravel footpath to the right from the old harbor. At Böcklerstrasse, cross to the right and continue down **Erkelenzdamm** to **Elizabeth-Hof** at #59–61. Elizabeth-Hof is typical of Kreuzberg's mixed residential and commercial complexes. Built in 1898, it not only contained large factories in the second and third courtyards but also housed residents from a variety of income groups. There is a lot of delivery traffic at this address, so watch your step as you make your way through the courtyards. In the first courtyard are the residential units. Here class differences become quickly apparent. The well-to-do lived in the *Vorderhaus*, above the front entrance, facing the street and the canal. These comfortable apartments were large, well lit, and appointed with full private baths, which you can identify by finding the large panes of plain frosted glass. (The large frosted windows with stained glass are stairwells.) More modest wage earners lived in the *Hinterhaus* at the rear of the courtyard. Their apartments were smaller, received less light, and had only small private

toilets, which were squeezed into a closet off the kitchen and were ventilated by a narrow frosted window, which you can see on every floor. The poorest residents lived in the *Seitenflügel*, the side wings. These much smaller apartments received almost no direct light, and residents had to share toilet facilities which were located between floors, as the narrow frosted ventilating windows to the side of the entrance doors indicate.

The factory owners of Elizabeth-Hof probably lived on the second and third floors of the *Vorderhaus*, white-collar employees in the *Hinterhaus*, and workers in the *Seitenflügel*. It must have been a difficult life to be constantly watched by employers who imposed a regimented industrial discipline; the clock at the end of the second courtyard is accompanied by the paternalistic exhortation: *Die Stunde ruft, Nütze die Zeit* (The hours chime, use the time). You'll see that the attractive green-and-white glazed tiling is missing in the third courtyard; the shop floors here were probably abandoned for a time in the 1960s. The walls were no longer heated, and the freezing temperatures cracked and destroyed the tile. By the 1970s, however, artists had rented out most of the lofts. As you turn around in the courtyard, you can still see the whimsical metal figure that advertised the talents of one sculptor. But most of the impoverished artists are gone now. With the fall of the Berlin Wall, the once isolated neighborhood of Kreuzberg has suddenly become centrally located and full of new money. As a result, rents have shot up, and computer and commercial entrepreneurs have moved in. The Kiez is gentrifying, which is yet another alternation in the volatile history of the city.

Exit Elizabeth-Hof and continue to the right down Erkelenzdamm. Before going too far, however, look back at Elizabeth-Hof. The giant indentation on the north wall clearly shows where a bomb fell during World War II; the empty lot next door probably indicates that a build

Fraenkelufer 38

ing was completely destroyed. Formerly an occupied building, or squat, the building at Erkelenzdamm 49 has been successfully modernized and features a bar, **Kühler Grund**, and a cafe, **Vierlinden**.

Walk a bit farther to Skalitzer Strasse, cross under the train tracks and continue on Erkelenzdamm to Oranienstrasse. As they make their way through the stone sea of tenement buildings, these elevated tracks follow the line of the old city walls. From Brandenburger Tor to Potsdamer Tor, onto Hallesches Tor at the end of Friedrichstrasse, and along here to Kottbusser Tor and Schlesisches Tor, the city wall enclosed those districts such as Friedrichstadt that had been laid out by the Great Elector Friedrich Wilhelm beyond the core of the old city. (Wassertorplatz is named after the *Wassertor*, or water gate, at which point the old city wall crossed the Luisenstädtischer Kanal.) Built in the 1730s to replace the obsolescent fortifications around medieval Berlin, the 10-foot-high *Akzisenmauer* (excise wall) allowed the king's agents to collect duties on all goods that entered the city and also kept conscripts garrisoned in the city from deserting. Desertion was a real problem, so much so that the king placed guards every twenty paces along the entire stretch of the wall. Even so, many peasant boys must have slipped out of their uniforms and out of the city. "The guards of the *Landwehr* are careful to examine farmers' wagons, making sure that no soldier without a pass has hidden himself on the same," read the daily orders of watchmen in January 1751. Guards were also told to make sure that "no soldier escapes dressed up as a woman." As late as 1803, homeowners near the wall were ordered to lock up their ladders at night. Thousands of youthful deserters did get out; and then, two hundred years later, many youths took up residence in this city in order to avoid conscription in the West German army.

The electric commuter railway that now crosses Er-

Sculpture at Elizabeth-Hof

kelenzdamm is almost a century old itself. The explosive growth of the city at the end of the nineteenth century required more mass transit, and the line here connected the southern and western precincts of the city with the *Stadtbahnring*. Siemens & Halske received the contract in 1896 but met with fierce opposition from neighbors who felt oppressed by the noise and unsightly iron bridgework of the railway. The complaints of mostly working-class Kreuzbergers did not interfere with construction of the line, however, which was completed in 1902. Nonetheless, when city fathers in the more affluent town of Charlottenburg (the district around the Kurfürstendamm that Berlin annexed in 1920) continued the line to Bahnhof Zoologischer Garten, they elected to build the electrical line underground. The high cost of tunneling through the wet sandy soil inflated subway ticket prices, which remained beyond the reach of most workers who preferred the slower but cheaper streetcars until the introduction of uniform prices on all mass transit in 1927.

As it travels over Gleisdreieck, Möckernbrücke, and on to Schlesisches Tor, the "Orient Express" (as U-Bahn line 1 is good-naturedly called on account of its destination to Turkish-accented Kreuzberg) has wonderfully appealing aspects. Commuters enjoy sunsets behind water towers, peer down at the old freight yards of the Anhalter Bahnhof, and are transformed into inadvertent voyeurs as they gaze into trackside apartment windows.

Berlin's mass transit is as tenacious as the city itself. Indeed, line 1 has been in operation without a major overhaul for nearly one hundred years. After World War II, the mauled U-Bahn and S-Bahn lines revived with astonishing speed. The relatively rapid economic reconstruction of Germany after World War II has always surprised foreigners, but it is important to realize how much of the city's infrastructure remained intact despite furious Allied bombing. Three-quarters of Berlin's one and a half million homes and apartments were damaged and two-fifths totally wrecked. Fifty thousand Berliners had been killed in the air raids. Berlin was now, in the words of Bertolt Brecht, simply a "rubble heap near Potsdam." Despite the extent of destruction, however, the first subway trains began running on May 14, 1945, only twelve days after the city's capitulation. By the end of May, 30 percent of the subway network was back in operation, carrying 170,000 passengers every day. When the wall divided East from West, the subways continued to ferry commuters below ground in East Berlin, past "ghost" subway stations—Stadtmitte, Französische Strasse, Oranienburger Strasse—empty except for the armed guards who stared mutely at the stylish West Berliners zipping past every three to five minutes.

As you walk along Erkelenzdamm toward Oranienplatz, you parallel the remains of the **Luisenstädtischer Kanal** on your left. Before World War II, an elegant neighborhood bordered the canal, but since then Kreuzberg has become more dilapidated and the canal has been filled in as a pleasant stretch of parkland. The canal was originally built as a work project to employ radical workers during the Revolution of 1848, and its fate has been closely tied to Germany's changing political landscape. The example of the February 1848 Revolution in Paris caught the imagination of ordinary Prussians, whose hopes for constitutional rights and civil liberties had been dashed after the Wars of Liberation. There was a political maxim: When France sneezes, the rest of Europe catches cold. On the evening of March 17, 1848, after much discussion of Parisian events, demonstrations in favor of a constitution erupted throughout Berlin. When the king's soldiers fired into the crowds, Berliners mobilized citizens' guards, assembled barricades, drove out the garrisoned soldiers, and occupied the city. Most of the fighting occurred in the city center, around Unter den Linden, Alexanderplatz, and the Gendarmenmarkt, but an arsenal was plundered near here at Hallesches Tor and a prison stormed and inmates liberated on Kreuzberg's Lindenstrasse. An eyewitness remembered the sense of republican unity that animated the entire city:

> Old and young, rich and poor joined together on every street corner to build these barriers. Booths, wagons, buses, carriages, huge freight, postal or farmers' carts, construction lumber—everything—were torn up, overturned, and brought together. Women and children worked alongside the rest. Everyone was equal. One saw, for example, two men carrying a beam, one of them in rags, the other in fine clothes. The basic materials used were torn-up paving stones, large boulders, beams, boards; to these were added beds hauled out of houses, along with sacks and other furniture. Everyone willingly contributed whatever he could. Women brought coffee, slices of bread, and handed food to the workers and fighters in the streets.

This magical moment of unity quickly faded, however. When workers demanded higher wages and a reduction of the work day to ten hours, the revolutionaries began to quarrel among themselves. According to the city council on April 23, 1848, "Journeymen, assistants, and workers have left their shops in the last days to attend public gatherings. They have even tried to disturb the labor of honest working men." In order to defuse a potentially explosive situation, city authorities proposed vast projects to put these rebellious demonstrators to work on Berlin's outskirts. These projects included the Luisenstädtischer Kanal. The canal would not only put "the dangerous classes" to work but once finished would offer workers the refinements of culture. "The more a people progresses culturally and economically," planners explained, "the greater their spiritual needs become. These include public walks." Laid out with elegant tree-lined concourses, the Luisenstädtischer Kanal would complement the Tiergarten and Unter den Linden as a place where "the diligent artisan and the busy factory worker could stroll in the evenings, after their day's work, and on Sundays."

As it was, Berlin workers were never as placated as city fathers hoped. Violent protests broke out even during construction of the canal. After engineers employed a steam pump to drain water from the excavation pit, workers burned the machine that they feared would make them redundant and erected a new set of barricades. This time, however, the rebels were opposed not by the king's soldiers but by the civil guard, which was called in to restore order. Fighting between the middle-class guards and workers on nearby Dresdener Strasse lasted until late in the evening of October 16, 1848. For historian Adolf Streckfuss, that night marked the end of the revolution: "A war between burghers and workers threatened to break out, a war among the people themselves, and just at a time when the reaction is gathering its strength to suppress this divided people." Less than a month later, on November 10, the archreactionary General Friedrich von Wrangel marched through the Brandenburger Tor at the head of a force of thirteen thousand soldiers. He re-established the king's tattered authority and suspended the rule of law.

The Luisenstädtischer Kanal was finally completed in 1852. Unfortunately, the canal silted up easily, residents dumped their garbage in the waters, and it gave off a foul smell. Most of the canal was filled in as a city-funded work project in 1926. War debris was later dumped into the remains of the canal. In 1982, the city finally employed workers to turn the former canal into a park, and after reunification in 1990, they began redigging the *Engelbecken*, or Angel Basin, an elegant reflecting pool that had been part of the canal. The pool is in front of Saint Michael's, a wartime ruin that can be seen ahead.

The grounds of the old canal continue to be sites of protest, however; **Oranienplatz** is the traditional starting-off point for Kreuzberg demonstrations. On May 1 and October 3, front lines that aren't so different from those in 1848 establish themselves, as riot police seal off the square filled with "dangerous classes" of stone-throwing anarchists.

At Oranienplatz, turn to the right and proceed along **Oranienburger Strasse**, a several-block stretch considered the main drag of Kreuzberg. We'll walk on the right for two colorful blocks and double back on the left as far as Adalbertstrasse.

Oranienstrasse is where you are most likely to see the "alternative" scene in action, especially in the afternoon and evening. Businesses come and go, especially since reunification. Still, the street is full of dark cafes, resale shops, bookstores, postmodern galleries, Turkish delicatessens, and smoky bars that still play *Schlager*, or German hits, from the 1950s. The Scheunenviertel (Walk 2) and Prenzlauer Berg (Walk 3) have stripped Kreuzberg of much of its status as the center of the "scene" as new money and new entrepreneurs slowly but surely change the face of this neighborhood. But places like **Frank's Billiard Salon** (open from 2 pm to 4 am) and the second-floor music club **Trash**, both in the first block on the left at Oranienstrasse 41, preserve the feel of the old Kiez. In the second block of "O-Strasse," **Elephantenpress** (at #25) is a Kreuzberg institution. The bookstore specializes in alternative, feminist, and local Berlin literature. A fine mixed-use building, **Oranien-Hof**, with three courtyards decorated in beige-and-green tile is located on the right-hand side of Oranienstrasse, at #183. Farther on there is a great junk shop, **Eichhörnchen** (#187). At night, Oranienstrasse comes into its own with all sorts of exotic inhabitants milling about the streets and in an equally exotic array of bars and cafes.

After two blocks, loop around Heinrichplatz, where well-groomed elderly Turkish men sip tea and coffee at **Dostlar Kiraathenesi** (#14), German neighbors drink beer in the kitschy **Zum Goldener Hahn** (#14a), and hipper Kreuzbergers order tequila at the Mexican cafe **Florian** (#17). Halfway back to Oranienplatz, at the busy corner of Adalbertstrasse, turn right.

Until 1989, Adalbertstrasse quickly led from the lively scene at Oranienstrasse to a series of increasingly quiet and isolated blocks that dead-ended at the wall. More and more traffic is returning, but Adalbertstrasse retains an old-fashioned aspect. The street is lined with handsome turn-of-the-century tenement buildings that were once so characteristic of Berlin. If you step into the large entryway at **#15**, you will find yourself on a rough cobblestoned courtyard surrounded by well-preserved brick stables and coachhouses. A more contemporary perspective awaits you at Waldemarstrasse, where, looking left, you see façades covered with whimsical graffiti and artwork.

Three blocks from Oranienstrasse, the street suddenly reveals an open strip, which is where the Berlin Wall used to divide Kreuzberg from the East Berlin district *Mitte*. The Gothic-style red-brick building across the way was in the East. Looking left, against the background of two tenement wings, lonely witnesses to the chopped-up postwar landscape of Berlin, you will find something completely unexpected: a **Kinderbauernhof**, or children's farm. The story of this inner-city farm on Bethaniendamm can have taken place only in Kreuzberg. The empty lot used to be simply another worthless piece of postwar property next to the wall. Enterprising parents decided to convert it to a small farm where city children could see more of the animal world than simply cats and dogs and sparrows. Here you will find goats, chickens, geese, pigs, lambs, and even ponies, all residing in a bucolic setting. In the 1980s, much as in the 1880s, Germans worried about losing their connection with the land. Forests, gardens, and parks are beloved spots for even the most metropolitan Berliner. (To this day, 17 percent of the area of Berlin consists of *Laubenkolonien*, garden plots that are carefully cultivated alongside railway corridors and tenaciously defended against real estate developers.) Although children from around Berlin came to pet the animals at this farm, the city suspected local organizers of having contacts with the violence-prone tenants' movement and even left-wing terrorists and were determined to forbid the farm's existence. Finally, a compromise was reached whereby the city of Berlin took over the farm as a kindergarten.

The very next day, one of the farm buildings burned down. The assumption was that anarchists had set it afire to protest the municipal takeover. It seemed that nothing could now prevent Berlin authorities from closing the farm altogether. When the police came, however, neighbors had organized a huge picnic breakfast on the grounds; coffee was being served, children played happily, and the police had no alternative but to back down in the face of all this merriment. Berliners had connived in similarly imaginative protests back in 1910 when Social Democrats obeyed the letter of a police prohibition against demonstrating for full voting rights by calling on their members to take a Sunday walk in the Tiergarten in ones and twos. Thousands of proletarian strollers crowded the park on March 6, 1910, and made a laughingstock of the Prussian police.

After the picnic coup, the urban farmers on Bethaniendamm decided to bring in a Native American shaman to help protect the ground from further encroachments by the authorities. He erected the hand-carved totem poles that you see on the four corners of the lot. And apparently his magic worked. An investigation later revealed that faulty electrical wiring rather than arson had been the cause of the mysterious fire—a report that saved the farm from further trouble. Only the straitened finances of the city of Berlin, which assists in the farm's expenses, threatens the future of this wonderful place.

Exit the farm on Adalbertstrasse, turn left, and then right onto Bethaniendamm, which follows the curve of the Luisenstädtischer Kanal, and head toward the very visible tower of Saint Thomas Kirche. Until 1989 the Berlin Wall—actually two walls divided by a wide security strip—ran right along Bethaniendamm. Here, Kreuzberg ended abruptly, right in the middle of the Cold War. On the east side, the wall was largely inaccessible to passers-

Kinderbauernhof

by and remained completely untouched. On the western side, however, it was possible to come right up to the 2.7-ton slabs, which were quickly transformed into urban canvases. When today's stylish coffee-table books and modish galleries include photos of the artwork and graffiti that decorated the west side of the wall, many of the examples came from politically and artistically active Kreuzbergers. Viewing the wall was a quick lesson in current events and political caricature, as well as a glimpse into the modern art scene. All this is gone now, although a few art books managed to catalog the evocative murals, and a brightly painted slab or two can be found in local museums (for example, see the Berlin Museum and Museum Haus am Checkpoint Charlie). The East Side Gallery near the main train station is composed of sections of the wall that were painted after November 1989 in an organized media event and has little in common with the anonymous and often angry Kreuzberg murals it tried to imitate.

Continue along Bethaniendamm to the back of **Saint Thomas Kirche**, a Protestant church built in 1864–69 in neo-Romanesque style by Friedrich Adler, a student of Schinkel, the greatest of Berlin architects (Walk 1). Just ahead you will see a **triangular section of garden** in the middle of an intersection that once abutted the wall. The small plot actually belonged to East Berlin, but East German authorities decided to leave it on the west side of the wall to save the expense of adding another twist and turn to the hundred-mile concrete serpent. For years this triangle of ground withered, but one day it caught the imagination of a Turkish immigrant, and he planted it with vegetables. Protected from the harsh northerly winds by the wall and, after much negotiation, tolerated by the East German border guards, the garden prospered. Eventually, the guards deeded the gardener his plot. Of course, this gift has no legal standing, but happily the garden still exists, although it is now exposed to the chilling north winds and an uncertain future.

Turn right off Bethaniendamm here, between the garden and the church. Just beyond the garden sits a stone **memorial** to the 122 students of the old Liebniz Gymnasium (next door) who died in World War I. A 1986 plaque puts this war monument in a historical context. It translates the patriotic Latin—"It is sweet and honorable to die for the fatherland"—and recalls the bitter past when such verses typically accompanied the death of young men; its contemporary message urges "Never again war."

Make your way around to the front of Saint Thomas. Ahead of you is the peaceful **Mariannenplatz**—a favorite neighborhood place for picnics, festivals, and outdoor theater. The last time we were there the big top—actually no more than 60 feet in diameter—was being raised. A small traveling circus with a half-dozen brightly colored wooden trailers and caravans had come to town. There was a wonderful, handcrafted magic about this circus on Mariannenplatz.

The large administrative building midway through the park on the right is **Künstlerhaus Bethanien**, a cultural center that provides German, Turkish, and visiting artists with grants and studio and gallery space. Bethanien's politics and blind spots are predictably far on the Left, but this Kreuzberg institution has been hugely successful in supporting local talent. It is open Tuesday through Sunday, 11 am to 6 pm.

In its former life, this brooding, Gothic-looking institution, with its eight-sided twin spires, was the former *Bethanien Hospital*, which opened in 1847 on what was then the muddy edge of the industrial city. Theodor Fontane, well known more for his novels than for his medicine, was employed here as a pharmacist during the revolutionary years 1848–49. Only thirty years later did Fontane finally begin writing the novels about old-fashioned Junkers (noblemen) and metropolitan nouveaux riches that established his reputation. There is still no better introduction to late-nineteenth-century Berlin

Künstlerhaus Bethanien

and to the surrounding province of Brandenburg than Fontane.

Make your way to Muskauer Strasse, directly opposite Bethanien. One of the best-known Turkish shops in Kreuzberg is located at the corner of Mariannenplatz and Muskauer Strasse (**#34**). Filiz Jureklek opened her clothing store, **Filiz Laden**, in 1983 after twenty years of laboring on Berlin's assembly lines. She is typical of many immigrants who decided to stay in Germany permanently, open their own businesses, and pridefully watch the professional successes of their children.

Next door, at **Muskauer Strasse #33**, is a Kreuzberg trade school in which apprentices who live on the premises learn construction, electrical work, and plumbing. A 1982 mural depicts the various crafts against the background of the neighborhood's restoration movement. Across Manteuffel Strasse, halfway down the block on the left, is a wood and coal dealer. On winter days residents pick up bundles of heating materials to feed their *Kachelofen*, or glazed tile ovens (Walk 3). If that does not work, the shop also sells bottles of beer and schnapps.

Continue along Muskauer Strasse to Pücklerstrasse; turn left and walk on the right-hand side of the street to the middle of the block. On the right, a red-brick **Markthalle**, an indoor market, recalls the subdued architectural style that Schinkel's students used until pushed aside by the monumental style of Wilhelm II's architects. The hall looks very much like an official building, and similarly designed schools, churches, social welfare institutions, and public buildings dotted late-nineteenth-century Berlin. According to the city's building superintendent Hermann Blankenstein, each official façade should convey the all-embracing authority of the Prussian state.

Blankenstein also imposed an increasingly functional and rational order on the sprawling city. Public toilets, bathhouses (like the one on Oderberger Strasse in Walk 3), and more potable water were all part of his hygienic agenda. Blankenstein also cleaned up the unsupervised and often dirty outdoor marketplaces by building fourteen of these market halls throughout Berlin, in addition to the central markets at Alexanderplatz (Walk 3), by 1893. A special police force was deputized to inspect produce and ensure its cleanliness, measures that outraged farmers and retailers who flinched at the omniscient "eye of the law." Not many of these halls survive, and this one is definitely worth a visit.

Built in 1890–91, the hall replaced the ostensibly unsanitary stalls of the outdoor market at Lausitzer Platz. It was municipal innovations such as the market halls that prompt historians today to refer to Berlin's "industrial culture" as the *Exerzierfeld*, or drill grounds, of the modern. This is a good place for a snack while contemplating the long arm of the rational state. The hall includes several places for a stand-up lunch, plus a wide assortment of produce, cheeses, prepared foods, Turkish specialties, fish, meats, and wursts. The hall also includes a supermarket, drugstore, and clothing shops.

Market halls like this, small neighborhood grocery stores, and weekly or biweekly outdoor markets such as the Turkish market on Maybacher Ufer at the beginning of the walk are an important part of the rhythm of daily life in Germany. As we have described, apartments throughout the city are often small and don't have room for large appliances or storage spaces. Thus, frequent shopping is a necessity for most families. Trips to outdoor markets with wicker baskets in hand or to supermarkets with hand-pulled carts are an everyday fact of life here. But timing, too, is important. Most neighborhood shops close their doors by 6 pm on weekdays and by 1 pm on Saturday. Except for flower shops, newspaper kiosks, and a few snack stands, nothing at all is open on Sunday. These strict hours are governed by national statutes and are intended to allow shopkeepers and their employees adequate time with their families. These hours also create a thoroughly peaceful atmosphere on Saturday and Sunday, although the burden of shopping in a timely fashion is hard on working mothers.

Walk through the hall to exit on Eisenbahnstrasse and turn left and then right at the corner to continue down Wrangelstrasse, named for the Prussian general who restored the authority of the Hohenzollerns in Berlin in the fall of 1848 and foreclosed on the democratic hopes of the revolution. At **#98**, an imposing mass of red brick signals another official building. Built in 1874–78, it housed one of the many regiments garrisoned in the city from the close of the Thirty Years' War to the end of World War I, almost three hundred years later. (Today, it is a trade school.) Given Kreuzberg's left-wing and antimilitarist reputation, it is ironic that the district once housed so many soldiers. Indeed, the main parade grounds of the monarchy were at *Tempelhof*, now an airport just south of Kreuzberg. At the beginning and end of every summer until the year 1919, a grand, full-dress military parade swept from the palace, down Unter den Linden and Friedrichstrasse, through Kreuzberg to Tempelhof, where the kaiser stood at the "solitary poplar tree" to review his troops. This glorious event attracted thousands of schoolchildren and patriots who lined the streets of the imperial capital.

Once you cross Skaltizer Strasse under the elevated train tracks, Wrangelstrasse grows much more lively. Shopkeepers shouting, children playing, and Turkish and German residents chatting all make the street feel pleasant and neighborly. At the corner you'll find several cafes and restaurants with outdoor tables. Farther on are Turkish-owned bakeries (*Firin*), butchers (*Kasap*), and vegetable stores (*Bakkal*). This part of Kreuzberg was not damaged either by wartime bombing or by postwar modernization and still has the appearance of a close-knit, turn-of-the-century neighborhood. Today, Turkish has replaced the Polish that was once widely spoken in Kreuzberg alongside German. The Kiez here begins to realize the utopia that renowned writer Günter Grass once imagined. "I envision Turkish, Croatian, Greek, and Italian city streets and city neighborhoods. Right next to Schultheiss [the big Kreuzberg brewery] I'd put in a mosque with a minaret. In the second generation, Turks, Croats, and Italians would be born and raised Berliners. They would have equal rights, would vote and be elected." Is this so utopian?

Proceed along Wrangelstrasse but take a look, on the right, into **Sorauer Strasse**, a classical proletarian street built by a single real estate developer, Paul Haberkern, in

1872–84. The handsome façades and large windows on the first and second storeys are deceptive. The roomy streetside apartments were usually rented by affluent civil servants, professionals, and tradesmen such as Haberkern, who lived on the next street over, at Lübbener Strasse 16. However, the apartments on the fourth and fifth storeys and in the backyard tenements had only one or two rooms in which as many as eight, nine, or even ten people lived. Haberkern's principle was to put as many people into as little space as possible. In the 1890s the Social Democratic newspaper *Vorwärts* estimated that even inmates in Plötzensee Prison had more room than tenants along this street. The result was unhygenic conditions, poor health, and lax morals. Places such as Sorauer Strasse conformed to Walter Benjamin's 1920s' definition of kitsch: "A working-class apartment behind a neo-Romanesque façade without a bath or toilet."

Today, the tenements have been much improved, though Sorauer Strasse still has the bare and stony atmosphere of proletarian Berlin. Here, the city really does appear to be a "sea of stone," which was a favorite image of early-twentieth-century Expressionist poets such as Georg Heym and Jakob von Hoddis. The street-front apartment buildings enclose not only impoverished backyard tenements but also schools and churches. The neighborhood grammar school for this area is in an interior courtyard at Skalitzer Strasse 55–56; another school and a Catholic church are in the middle of the next block (the entrance to the church is on Wrangelstrasse, just ahead). If you wish, take a look into the long narrow courtyard that stretches the length of the entire block at Sorauer Strasse 5 or 9.

Who used to live on Sorauer Strasse? An 1893 report counted 771 gainfully employed persons whose trades revealed Berlin to be a capital of industry and manufacturing. In addition to 266 unskilled workers, there were 70 cabinetmakers, 37 masons, 24 locksmiths, 16 shoemakers, 15 carpenters, 14 coachmen, 12 seamstresses, 11 painters, 10 turners, 9 merchants, 6 plumbers and blacksmiths, 5 tailors, 5 coopers, 5 beltmakers, 5 taxi drivers, 4 railway workers, 4 milkmen, 4 innkeepers, 4 butchers, 4 molders, 4 coppersmiths, 4 lithographers, 3 shopkeepers, 3 bakers, 3 polishers, 3 upholsterers, 3 pipefitters, 3 firemen, 3 rentiers, 2 civil servants, 2 policemen, 2 mailmen, 2 invalids, 2 streetcar drivers, 2 vegetable merchants, 2 gardeners, 2 hairdressers, 2 wagon drivers, 2 potters, 2 roofers, 2 construction workers, 2 stucco workers, 2 goldsmiths, 2 wheelwrights, 2 box makers, 2 leather workers, 2 saddle makers, 2 stokers, 2 machinists, 2 mechanics, 2 cigar makers, 2 conductors, 2 waiters, and 2 organ grinders, as well as a secretary, post office employee, usher, watchman, locomotive driver, brakeman, streetcar worker, grain dealer, baker's assistant, beer brewer, miller, fisherman, furniture dealer, sculptor, frame maker, piano factory worker, lace maker, building contractor, poster hanger, ivory carver, basket maker, machine tender, lumberman, brush maker, clock maker, metal pressman, dyemaker, sievemaker, printer, cigarette worker, gas worker, public weigher, scribe, messenger, butler, street sweeper, and button maker.

Most of these workers were newly arrived immigrants from Brandenburg and Silesia, and many were Poles. Around here one found not only Social Democratic and Catholic pubs but also variations in Polish and German. Catholic churches in this part of Kreuzberg offered services in Polish as well as German. Today, this neighborhood features street-front gaming rooms for Turkish men and mosques housed in back courtyard apartments.

From Sorauer Strasse, walk another block down Wrangelstrasse, turn left onto Oppelner Strasse, and you will quickly arrive at **Schlesisches Tor**. A magnificent commuter station, completely restored in neo-Romanesque style with a charming onion dome, dominates the busy intersection. Despite the fact that the train tracks continue, this is the end of the subway line, which will get you home, or stop here for refreshments. The **Bagdad Cafe**, across from the station, with its welcoming summer garden, is the place to go.

Museums,
Restaurants,
Hotels,
and Shops

MUSEUMS

You could spend days without end in Berlin's magnificent assortment of museums, exploring everything from masterpieces of antiquity to the most avant-garde work of today's artists. Your selection, then, will depend on how much time you have and where your interests lie. Our own particular favorites are listed below (along with museums mentioned in the four walks), but for a complete listing of the city's museums and special exhibits, you should pick up a guide, *Tip* or *Zitty*. A special *Tageskarte* (day ticket) costing 8 DM will gain you admittance to many of the state-run museums; admittance on Sunday and holidays is free. Pick up a brochure or inquire at the cashier's desk for a complete list of the museums included. Except where otherwise noted, admission to all museums is 4 DM.

Museums are scattered throughout the city, but Berlin also boasts several concentrations of culture—the Museumsinsel, the Dahlem Complex, and Schloss Charlottenburg—with convenient groupings of museums. If you want to spend an afternoon or a day doing museums but don't want to criss-cross the city, you could pick one of these areas and focus your attention there.

MUSEUMSINSEL: Located in the heart of Berlin's Mitte district, this island contains the Pergamonmuseum, Bode Museum, Altes Museum, and the Alte Nationalgalerie. The most famous and worthy of these is the Pergamon, although each museum houses interesting collections. The easiest way to get here is to take bus #100 or the S-Bahn to Hackescher Markt.

Pergamonmuseum: Named for the famous temple that is housed here, this museum contains spectacular examples of early Grecian, Roman, and Babylonian architecture—not just the massive temple altar from a site now in Turkey but soaring Roman market gates, and the impressive Babylonian gates of Ishtar have been erected inside the museum—as well as pottery and decorative arts from the Middle East and the Orient. Open daily 9 am to 5 pm; however on Monday and Tuesday only the architectural hall is open.

Alte Nationalgalerie: Not to be confused with the Neue Nationalgalerie, which is in West Berlin, this museum features paintings and sculpture from the nineteenth and twentieth centuries. Here you will find some good examples of the artwork of the Berlin Secessionists Max Liebermann, Otto Dix, Ernst Ludwig Kirchner, and Emil Nolde, among others. Open Wednesday to Sunday, 9 am to 5 pm.

Altes Museum: This museum, designed by Karl Friedrich Schinkel (see Walk 1), contains no permanent exhibits; rather, it is used as a special exhibition hall. Current shows are advertised on posters outside the museum. Variable opening times.

DAHLEM MUSEUM COMPLEX: Tucked out of the way in a prosperous neighborhood of single-family homes and villas on the edge of the Grunewald, this museum complex was established in the postwar years and rivals the Museumsinsel in the impressive breadth and depth of its collections. With reunification, however, some collections are being relocated. At this writing, the complex has the following museums open to the public: Gemäldegalerie, Museum für Indische Kunst; Museum für Islamische Kunst; Museum für Ostasiatische Kunst; Museum für Völkerkunde; and the Skulpturengalerie.

The main museum center has its entrances on Arnimallee and Lansstrasse but another museum that shouldn't be overlooked, the Museum für Deutsche Volkskunde, sits several blocks away. The easiest way to get here is to take the U-Bahn to Dahlem-Dorf and follow the signs to the museums of your choice; they are all within a five-minute walk of the station. Staatliche Museen, Lansstrasse 8 (Dahlem). Open daily except Monday, 9 am to 5 pm; Saturday and Sunday, 10 am to 5 pm. Entrance fee: 4 DM for adults for admission to all museums in the complex.

Gemäldegalerie (Picture Gallery): This museum contains an impressive collection of paintings by European artists from the thirteenth to the eighteenth centuries, including Rembrandt, Brueghel, Dürer, Vermeer, Rubens, Gainsborough, Titian, Botticelli, Caravaggio, El Greco, and Goya, just to name a few.

Museum für Indische Kunst (Museum for Indian Art): A historically rich assortment of artwork covering four thousand years and including works from the Indian subcontinent, Himalayan countries, and Central and Southeast Asia. The beautiful displays include ceramic, stone, and bronze sculptures, figurines, and implements, as well as carved objects in wood, jade, and ivory, painted texts, textiles, and wall murals from Buddhist cave monasteries of Central Asia.

Museum für Islamische Kunst (Museum of Islamic Art): Dominated by impressive carpets, this exceptional museum also includes fine examples of the Koran, plus ceramics, glass, jewelry, and ornamental objects, many of which are decorated with quotations from the Koran.

Museum für Ostasiatische Kunst (Museum of Far Eastern Art): Including fine and decorative arts from China, Japan, and Korea, the museum has examples of early bronze and ceramic ware (some pieces dating to the twelfth century B.C.), plus exquisite examples of screen painting, lacquer ware, hanging scrolls, color woodcuts, and some contemporary examples of these ancient arts.

Museum für Völkerkunde (Museum of Ethnography): Only a portion of this museum's extensive ethnographic holdings from around the world can be displayed here, but the future relocation plans should allow for a greater portion of their collections to be on view. The largest exhibits are in the Oceanian department, which includes original dwellings and large boats, and the American Archaeology department, which houses an immense collection of pre-Columbian artifacts from Mexico and Peru. Smaller exhibits from the East Asia, South Asia, Africa, and Music Ethnology departments are also on display.

Skulpturengalerie (Sculpture Gallery): This large collection of sculptures, beginning with the Early Christian–Byzantine period and continuing through the eighteenth century, focuses primarily on the history of European religious and figurative sculpture.

Museum für Volkskunde (Museum of Folk Customs): Containing a wide array of household items such as dowry furniture, clothing, cookware, dolls, toys, and other playthings, this museum gives a fascinating glimpse into typical German family life from the sixteenth century to the present. Im Winkel 6–8. Open daily, except Monday, 9 am to 5 pm; Saturday and Sunday, 10 am to 5 pm.

SCHLOSS CHARLOTTENBURG: Clustered around an impressively redone baroque palace that sits on the bank of the Spree River, the various museums here, plus the palace's formal gardens, make for an enticing cultural getaway in the heart of a bustling metropolis. Across the street from the palace are three other museums worth visiting: the Egyptian Museum, the Museum of Greek and Roman Antiquities, and the Bröhan Museum.

There are many more possible sights to see in the palace or on the grounds than we have mentioned, and you should feel free explore all the offerings. Our favorites are the *Galerie der Romantik*, which contains some impressive examples of paintings by German Romantic masters such as Caspar David Friedrick, and the *Schinkel Pavilion*, a delightful summer palace designed by Karl Friedrich Schinkel and filled with an interesting assortment of artwork. If you are interested in rococco-style furnishings and decorative architecture, you can stroll through the rooms in the Knobelsdorff-Flügel (new wing of the palace). Schloss Charlottenburg, Spandauer Damm. Open Tuesday to Sunday, 10 am to 5 pm. The entrance fee varies according to the sights to be included in the visit; the gallery and grounds can be visited for free.

Aegyptisches Museum (Egyptian Museum): This small but beautifully arranged museum, is perhaps best known for the exquisite bust of Queen Nefertiti, but certainly that is not the only item of significance here. The museum also contains numerous sarcophagi, a mummy, and other burial items, busts of other Egyptian royalty, and the Kalabasha Gate. Schlossstrasse 70 (Charlottenburg). Open Monday to Thursday, 9 am to 5 pm; Saturday and Sunday, 10 am to 5 pm.

Antikenmuseum (Museum of Greek and Roman Antiquities): This is an extraordinarily fine collection of early Greek, Roman, and Etruscan pottery and sculpture and other assorted artwork, including beautiful early jewelry. Schlossstrasse 1 (Charlottenburg). Open Monday to Thursday, 9 am to 5 pm; Saturday and Sunday, 10 am to 5 pm.

Bröhan Museum: If the graceful, sweeping lines of art nouveau–, or *Jugendstil*-style furnishings and decorative artwork such as glassware, ceramics, jewelry, and painting, or the spare, modern look of the art deco movement capture your fancy, you owe it to yourself to visit this privately owned museum next to the Antikenmuseum. Room after room of period furnishings instill a sense of awe at turn-of-the-century craftmanship. Schlossstrasse la (Charlottenburg). Open Tuesday to Sunday, 10 am to 6 pm. Entrance fee, 3 DM.

Käthe Kollwitz Museum: This small gallery housed on several floors of a beautiful turn-of-the-century villa is a moving testament to the evocative power of Kollwitz's art. Her life was explored briefly on Walk 3 (Prenzlauer Berg); here, you can see her working-class neighbors and other subjects powerfully depicted. Fasanenstrasse 24. Open daily except Tuesday, 11 am to 6 pm. Entrance fee, 6 DM.

Neue Nationalgalerie: Enclosed in an airy glass-and-steel structure designed by Mies van der Rohe, this impressive collection of nineteenth- and twentieth-century paintings is harmoniously situated. Among the reasons to visit here is to see the exemplary work of German Secessionists and Expressionists such as Ernst Ludwig Kirchner, Otto Dix, and George Grosz. A cautionary note: The museum does not have adequate room to exhibit much of their collection when a special show is installed downstairs; we recommend you call in advance to see if any of the museum is closed off (tel: 266 26 51). Potsdamer Strasse 50. Open Tuesday through Friday, 9 am to 5 pm; Saturday and Sunday, 10 am to 5 pm.

Museum für Verkehr und Technik (Museum of Traffic and Technology): A fascinating assemblage of steam-powered tooling machines; factory equipment, such as that used for textile manufacture or suitcase production; printing presses; early computer technology; and assorted vehicles, such as early bicycles, motorcycles, automobiles, and airplanes. But best of all are the trains: Housed in the old train yard switching stations that are attached to the rest of the museum, three huge rooms (designated *Lokschuppen*) are filled with locomotives and

Altes Museum

coaches, from the earliest steam engines to modern examples of the *Deutsche Bundesbahn*. Stairs and platforms let the curious peek in and around these massive and impressive machines. A wonderful place for both adults and children to explore. The best way to get here is to take the U-Bahn to Möckernbrücke. Trebbiner Strasse 9 (Kreuzberg). Open Tuesday to Friday, 9 am to 5:30 pm; Saturday and Sunday, 10 am to 6 pm. Entrance fee, 3.50 DM.

Bauhaus Archiv: Filled with samples of Bauhaus furnishings, decorative pieces, architectural plans, paintings, and photographs, this museum is an exciting place to encounter the work of Gropius, Klee, Kandinsky, Mies van der Rohe, and Moholy-Nagy, among others. Klingelhöferstrasse 13–14 (at the edge of the Landwehrkanal between Reichpietschufer and Lützowufer). Open Wednesday to Monday, 10 am to 5 pm.

Berlin Museum: Dedicated to depicting the life and history of Berlin, this museum houses collections covering politics, cultural life, and middle-class households. Two intact sections of the Berlin Wall have also been placed on display here. Models of the city's early development are helpful guides to understanding Berlin's tumultuous growth and transformation. This museum includes a working pub! Lindenstrasse 14 (Kreuzberg). Open Tuesday through Sunday, 10 am to 8 pm.

Topographie des Terrors: Stresemannstrasse 110 and a back entrance on Wilhelmsstrasse at Kochstrasse. Open daily, 10 am to 6 pm. Admission is free.

Museum Haus am Checkpoint Charlie: Friedrichstrasse 44 (Mitte). Open daily, 9 am to 10 pm. Entrance fee, 4 DM. (Be sure you see the exhibits in both wings of the museum.)

Huguenot Museum: Französischer Dom on the Gendarmenmarkt. Open Monday through Saturday, 12 pm to 5 pm, and Sunday, 1 pm to 5 pm. Entrance fee, 2 DM.

Schinkel Museum: Friedrichswerder Kirche, Werderstrasse (Mitte). Open Wednesday through Sunday, 9 am to 5 pm. Entrance fee, 4 DM.

Museum of German History: Zeughaus, Unter den Linden 2. This museum is scheduled to open in 1995.

Friseurmuseum (Hairdressing Museum): Husemannstrasse 8. Open daily, 10 am to 4 pm, with extended hours on Tuesday, Wednesday, and Thursday until 5 pm and on Saturday until 6 pm. Entrance fee, 2 DM.

Museum Berliner Arbeiterleben um 1900 (Museum of Working-class Life Around 1900): Husemannstrasse 12. Open Tuesday through Saturday, 10 am to 6 pm, except Friday when the museum closes at 3 pm. Entrance fee, 2 DM.

RESTAURANTS

In addition to the selection of restaurants listed below, visitors will find a dense concentration of establishments around Savignyplatz and on the streets extending south from there, particularly along Grolmanstrasse and Knesebeckstrasse. Also, on the sixth floor of *KaDeWe*, the Wittenbergplatz department store (open Monday to Friday, 9 am to 6:30 pm; Saturday, 9 am to 2 pm), features a dozen food bars offering regional as well as international fare with a dazzling array of fresh and prepared specialties. Even if you are not hungry, don't miss the chance to survey the numerous meat counters featuring an infinite variety of wursts, smoked meats, and cold cuts.

Carmers: Carmerstrasse 2. Tel: 312 31 15. A Berlin favorite with excellent continental cuisine at higher-end prices.

Lutter & Wegner: Schlüterstrasse 55. Tel: 881 34 40. Named after the famous Berlin winery, this refined, dark-paneled restaurant serves well-prepared German food.

Cour Carrée: Savignyplatz 5. Tel. 312 52 38. A popular bistro serving continental food. There is a lovely large outdoor garden for summer evening meals.

Reste Fidele: Bleibtreustrasse 41. Tel: 881 16 05. Continental food with French and Italian touches in a very congenial atmosphere, with lots of outdoor seating.

Shell: Knesebeckstrasse 22. Tel: 312 83 20. Just north of Savignyplatz, this bistro is open from morning until late at night, serving coffee, drinks, and well-prepared meals to a diverse, rather stylish crowd.

Weinstube am Savignyplatz: Savignyplatz 11 (entrance on Kantstrasse). Tel: 313 86 97. Excellent Alsatian food in the evening.

Hardtke: Meinikestrasse 27. Tel: 881 98 27. Traditional but attentively prepared German food in a comfortable setting. Regrettably, no credit cards are accepted.

Cafe Hardenberg: Hardenbergstrasse 10. Tel: 312 26 44. This crowded and popular student cafe is a great place to sit and people-watch while feasting on a late breakfast. Light meals and diverse salads and sandwiches are available as well.

Wintergarten: Fasanenstrasse 23. Tel: 882 54 14. This casually elegant cafe, just off the Ku'damm on a quiet street lined with art nouveau buildings, has delightful garden seating in addition to rooms inside the build-

Operncafe

ing attached to the Literaturhaus. The cafe is next door to the Käthe Kollwitz Museum and is a nice place to start the day with breakfast, to pause for lunch, or to rejuvenate yourself with coffee and cake in the late afternoon.

Filmbühne am Steinplatz: Hardenbergstrasse 12. Tel: 312 90 12. A good place for breakfast, coffee, newspaper browsing, or a light meal.

Cafe Möhring: Kurfürstendamm 213 (Tel: 881 20 75); Kurfürstendamm 234 (Tel: 882 38 44); and on the Gendarmenmarkt (Tel: 209 022 44). Möhring was one of the few old and famous cafes of the 1920s to survive World War II. The original owners have since passed on, and new branches can be found throughout Berlin. Nonetheless, the elegant atmosphere and appealing pastries and desserts have remained with the name. If fruit desserts appeal to you, don't miss the Rote Grütze, a tart-sweet compote of red currants, raspberries, cherries, and other red seasonal fruits.

Surya: Grolmannstrasse 22. Tel: 312 91 23. Superb Indian food, friendly service, and decent prices.

Angora. Schlüterstrasse 29. Tel: 323 70 96. Decorated with Assyrian-style stone wall reliefs, this is a relaxing and untouristy place to come for well-prepared Turkish food. Appetizers are a particularly wonderful aspect of Turkish dining, and you should try a combination platter for an excellent introduction.

Mundart: Muskauer Strasse 33–34. Tel: 612 20 61. Tucked away in a residential Kreuzberg street, Mundart serves imaginative French food at reasonable prices.

Henne: Leuschnerdamm 25. Tel: 614 77 30. A classic neighborhood restaurant with a citywide reputation for roast chicken, Henne is open only in the evening after 7, except Monday and Tuesday. Dinner reservations are accepted after 6 pm.

In East Berlin try the following:

Restaurant Borchardt: Französischestrasse 47. Tel: 229 31 44. Airy and elegant, this very upscale establishment just off the Gendarmenmarkt has a diverse and well-prepared menu featuring German and continental cuisine.

Operncafe: Unter den Linden 5. Tel: 238 40 16. The Operncafe combines wonderful brunches, a spectacular display of mouth-watering pastries, and a first-class restaurant in an elegant setting right on Unter den Linden. The cafe is reached by entering the building, but one can be seated either inside or on the outdoor terrace. The busy outdoor cafe in front of the building is self-service and not part of the same establishment, but it is highly recommended as a place for a grilled wurst and a Berliner Weisse.

Bistro 1900: Husemannstrasse 2. Tel: 449 40 52. This small, comfortable bistro on Käthe-Kollwitz-Platz serves well-prepared German and continental dishes. The bar becomes quite crowded in the evening.

Oren: Oranienburger Strasse 28. Tel: 282 82 28. Since opening a few years ago, Oren has established a sturdy and well-deserved reputation for light German and Middle Eastern dishes. In the heart of the Scheunenviertel and near the Museumsinsel, Oren can get quite crowded.

HOTELS

Staying in West Berlin near the Kurfürstendamm and Savignyplatz is still by far the best way to enjoy Berlin; thus, our recommendations concentrate in this area. At any of the following establishments you will be near a huge array of restaurants and shops and have easy access to public transportation.

Although the commercial districts of East Berlin are reviving quickly, the neighborhoods remain relatively lifeless and don't have much to entertain tourists. If you are interested in staying in the East, however, we recommend the hotels around the Gendarmenmarkt where there are also several restaurants and convenient public transportation. Our choices would be either the *Hilton*, Mohrenstrasse 30 (Tel: 238 20), or *Charlottenhof*, Charlottenstrasse 52 (Tel: 203 566 00). The fancy (and very expensive) *Grand Hotel* on Friedrichstrasse receives a lot of press but leaves us cold.

One of the first things tourists notice about Berlin is the high price of accommodations and the difficulty of finding a room during the summer months. If you need assistance finding a hotel when you arrive, pay a visit to the *Verkehrsamt* (Berlin Tourist Office), which has offices at Bahnhof Zoologischer Garten, the Europa Center, Alexanderplatz, and Tegel Airport. You will find that first-class hotels here are superb but very expensive. At the other end of the scale, we find the pensions on Fasanenstrasse very reasonable with an old-world graciousness. The recommended selections below are listed in order of descending price.

Grand Hotel Esplanade Berlin: Lützowufer 15.

Tel: 261 01 10. A dazzlingly designed hotel overlooking the Landwehrkanal, the Esplanade offers a full range of services and rooms. Guests can use bicycles free of charge.

Hotel Steigenberger Berlin: Los-Angeles-Platz 1. Tel: 210 80. An elegant and luxurious five-star hotel on a quiet square just off Tauentzienstrasse between Wittenbergplatz and the Kurfürstendamm.

Savoy Hotel: Fasanenstrasse 9–10. Tel: 311 030. A first-rate hotel with understated class.

Arosa Parkschloss Hotel: Lietzenburger Strasse 79–81. Tel: 880 05 50. Well run and very comfortable.

Hotel Lenz: Xantener Strasse 8. Tel: 881 51 58. Well located just off Olivaerplatz, Hotel Lenz is a charming choice at modest prices.

Hotel Residenz: Meineckestrasse 9. Tel: 88 44 30. A charming and reliable hotel.

Hotel-Pension Fasanenhaus: Fasanenstrasse 73. Tel: 881 67 13. With a wonderful location on the elegant Fasanenstrasse, this pension has large and comfortable rooms in a turn-of-the-century building. Together with Pension Funk, listed below, this is a personal favorite.

Hotel-Pension Funk: Fasanenstrasse 69. Tel: 882 71 93. If you want to stay a little bit off the beaten track, try **Riehmers Hofgarten**, Yorckstrasse 83 (Tel: 78 10 11). In a fashionable Kreuzberg neighborhood, Riehmers is a comfortable hotel with reasonable prices.

SHOPS

Berlin is a huge city with an enormous selection of fashionable stores and boutiques. Rather than choosing a few establishments we have suggested a number of shopping areas that can be easily browsed. Most shops are open Monday through Friday from 10 am to 6 pm and on Saturday from 10 am to 1 pm. Irritatingly, few specialty stores remain open until 6 pm on "long Saturdays," which fall on the first Saturday of every month.

The **Kurfürstendamm** remains Berlin's indispensable boulevard for the shopper. From Joachimsthaler Strasse, past the Kaiser-Wilhelm-Gedächtniskirche, all the way to Olivaerplatz, the Ku'damm is lined with shops, galleries, and department stores. Be sure to explore the side streets, particularly Fasanenstrasse and, north of the Ku'damm, Bleibtreustrasse and Schlüterstrasse.

Shops also line the passage beneath the S-Bahn on either side of **Savignyplatz**. Here you will find *Bücherbogen*, snuggled in arches numbered 592 to 594, one of the world's best stores for art and architectural books.

Fine **antique stores** can be found throughout West Berlin, but a number are clustered along Fasenenstrasse, Schlüterstrasse, and Keithstrasse. The well-known antique market once located at Nolldendorfplatz has moved into the S-Bahn arches just north of Bahnhof Friedrichstrasse—and it is open on Sunday! For antique books there is no equal to the blocks around Motzstrasse and Winterfeldstrasse. Antiques of varying quality, secondhand goods of all sorts, and handmade arts and crafts can be found any weekend at the large outdoor flea market by the Tiergarten S-Bahn station on Strasse des 17 Juni. Handmade crafts and delightful toys, plus assorted antiques and secondhand goods, can also be found weekends at the outdoor market beside the Spree in front of the Museumsinsel, and diagonally across the street behind the Operncafe.

For a big selection of reasonably priced **ceramic dishware** glazed in a predominantly blue pattern typical of central Germany, visit *Bunzlauer Bauerngeschirr* at Hohenzollerndamm 197, which is just across the street from the Hohenzollerndamm stop on the U-Bahn. Open Tuesday to Friday, 11 am to 6 pm; Saturday, 10 am to 1 pm.

Berlin's world-famous department store **KaDeWe**,

which stands for *Kaufhaus des Westens*, opened on Wittenbergplatz at the beginning of the century to serve the new rich in the western districts. It has survived inflation, the Great Depression, and world wars, and while it offers a full range of wares, in the end it is rather conventional. What deserves your special attention, however, is the food emporium on the sixth floor and the year-round Christmas section on the fourth floor that sells the wooden ornaments, candle wreaths, and music boxes typical of Germany.

The best place to buy **books** is the sprawling *Kiepert* store at Hardenbergstrasse 4–5. Kiepert and *Marga Schoeller*, Knesebeckstrasse 33–34, have the best selection of English-language books; the *British Bookstore* at Mauerstrasse 83 (near Checkpoint Charlie) has a large selection as well. Bibliophiles will want to wander in the cramped aisles of the *Heinrich Heine Buchhandlung*, beneath Bahnhof Zoologischer Garten on Hardenbergstrasse—this is a Berlin original.

Berlin has wonderful **outdoor food markets**. For more than a hundred years, Winterfeldplatz has been the site of a Saturday morning fresh food market that draws shoppers from around Berlin. The Turkish market on Maybacher Ufer in Kreuzberg, open on Tuesday and Friday, features many typically Turkish foods. At Christmastime, charming outdoor markets at Breitscheidplatz (at the beginning of the Ku'damm around the *Gedächtniskirche*) and in Spandau sell trinkets, jewelry, mulled wine, and other winter specialities. Try to avoid the weekend crowds.

As for East Berlin, the selections still remain limited. A number of artisanal shops and galleries are opening in the Scheunenviertel, however, particularly on Ackerstrasse and Sophienstrasse.

Index

Index

Index

THE HENRY HOLT WALKS SERIES

For people who want to *learn* when they travel, not just see.

Look for these other exciting volumes in Henry Holt's best-selling Walks series:

PARISWALKS, Revised Edition, by Alison and Sonia Landes
Five intimate walking tours through the most historic quarters of the City of Light.
288 pages, photos, maps $12.95 Paper

LONDONWALKS, Revised Edition, by Anton Powell
Five historic walks through old London, one brand-new for this edition.
272 pages, photos, maps $12.95 Paper

VENICEWALKS by Chas Carner and Alessandro Giannatasio
Four enchanting tours through one of the most perfect walking environments the world has to offer.
240 pages, photos, maps $12.95 Paper

FLORENCEWALKS, Revised Edition, by Anne Holler
Four intimate walks through this exquisite medieval city, exploring its world-famous art and architecture.
240 pages, photos, maps $12.95 Paper

VIENNAWALKS, Revised Edition, by J. Sydney Jones
Four walking tours that reveal the homes of Beethoven, Freud, and the Habsburg monarchy.
304 pages, photos, maps $12.95 Paper

RUSSIAWALKS by David and Valeria Matlock
Seven intimate tours—four in Moscow and three in Leningrad—that explore the hidden treasures of these enigmatic cities.
304 pages, photos, maps $12.95 Paper

NEW YORKWALKS by The 92nd Street Y, edited by Batia Plotch
One of the city's most visible cultural and literary institutions guides you through six historic neighborhoods in New York.
336 pages, photos, maps $12.95 Paper

BARCELONAWALKS by George Semler
Five walking tours through Spain's cultural and artistic center—synonymous with such names as Gaudí, Miró, and Picasso.
272 pages, photos, maps $12.95 Paper

JERUSALEMWALKS, Revised Edition, by Nitza Rosovsky
Six intimate walks that allow the mystery and magic of this city to unfold.
304 pages, photos, maps $14.95 Paper

BEIJINGWALKS by Don J. Cohn and Zhang Jingqing
Six intimate walking tours of the most historic quarters of this politically and culturally complex city.
272 pages, photos, maps $15.95 Paper

ROMEWALKS, Revised Edition, by Anya Shetterly
Five walking tours through the most historically and culturally rich neighborhoods of Rome.
320 pages, photos, maps $14.95 Paper

MADRIDWALKS by George Semler
Five extraordinary walking tours that uncover the many architectural treasures and historical secrets of this glorious city.
284 pages, photos, maps $14.95 Paper

PRAGUEWALKS by Ivana Edwards
Five walking tours through this magical city.
288 pages, photos, maps $14.95 Paper